A PORTRAIT OF
BISHOP OTTER COLLEGE

CHICHESTER
1839-1990

by
Heather Warne and
Trevor Brighton

West Sussex Institute of Higher Education 1992.

ISBN O 948765 63 1

Printed by RPM Reprographics Ltd in association with Newline Graphics.

© July 1992.

Contents

ACKNOWLEDGEMENTS

The authors would like to thank the Trustees of Bishop Otter College for enabling the College archives to be catalogued and for providing funds for this publication. Equal thanks are extended to the W.I.S.H.E. Research and Publication Committee for their contribution towards the production costs of this book.

We regret that the restraints on text in a photographic publication have made it impossible for us to mention all those persons, past and present, who have made a significant contribution to the history of the College and we therefore apologise for any omissions.

We should like to thank Scott Robertson and the Library staff for providing Library space while this book was in preparation: and all the staff and students, too numerous to mention individually, who helped in the various activities of the 150th year and in staging the 150th exhibition. We remember, with grateful appreciation, the curatorial assistance of the late Brian Wigmore during the three months that the exhibition ran. Finally, we thank Jo Shepherdson, Sarah Davey and Tracey Bruton for typing the text of this book.

The Oriel Window above the Cloisters.

The carving depicts the arms of the see of Chichester impaling those of William Otter, beneath a mitre. The rebus beneath shows an otter devouring an eel or a serpent. In the spandrels of the arch are carved G O (eps.) - Gulielmus Otter episcopus. The translated Latin inscription reads:

This College, for training teachers of the poor children of this diocese, was erected as a memorial of the piety of the most worthy Bishop William Otter STP, in the year of our Saviour 1850.

THE COLLEGE ARCHIVES AND THIS BOOK

Bishop Otter College is fortunate in possessing an excellent series of archives, both manuscript and photographic, dating from the middle of the nineteenth century. From time to time this resource has yielded its secrets to those who have wished to probe the history of the College and as a result some very useful studies have emerged, not least *Bishop Otter College and Policy for Teacher Education 1839-1980*, published in 1981 by former Principal, Gordon McGregor.

In 1988 it was decided that the 150th anniversary of the foundation of the College, due to fall in 1989, should be acknowledged in various ways. Whatever form the 150th celebrations might eventually take, it was felt that nothing should be done without first looking seriously at the College archives themselves. But how should this be tackled? The archives, though safely stored within the College library, were uncatalogued, and were, therefore, a largely-unknown resource. There was no one within the College whose schedule could accommodate a task of nature and I was therefore engaged in the academic year 1988 - 1989 for the purpose of cataloguing the College archives.

Time ran out, as it usually does, before the frills and furbelows could be attended to, and before a typed and printed catalogue could be produced, but by May 1989, I had catalogued not only the manuscript archives, but also upwards of 3,000 photographs. I then 'borrowed' **Bernard Vick**, a long-standing resident of Chichester who gives his valuable spare time to cataloguing the Diocesan records at West Sussex record Office. With Bernard's help, while the Diocesan records waited, Bishop Otter College's records were all numbered, boxed and made readily identifiable and retrievable, should the need arise to consult them.

The need indeed arose. The new Mitre Art Gallery had been recently opened and the 150th celebrations would not be complete, it was decided, without a photographic exhibition of the College's history, filling the new gallery from top to toe. I was hastily re-summoned and immediately set to work. By degrees and with the help of College staff, the story was pieced together - the early days of the men's College, the reopening in 1873, life in 'the dorm', new science labs, embellishments to the chapel: all facets and stages of College history had been faithfully recorded by the camera's eye. These were not the sophisticated cameras of today. The photographers were often the students themselves, capturing a much-loved aspect of the chapel or cloister or posing with a group of their special friends, creating the desired memento for their album and for later years.

With the help of **Sue Elliot**, WSIHE's photographer, small, faded sepia shots dating from the Victorian and Edwardian periods were transformed into 8" by 10" reprints suitable for exhibition. The opening of the exhibition was timed to coincide with the reunion weekend, 16th - 17th June 1990, the high spot and finale of a year of 150th celebrations. I was nervously aware that I, a complete newcomer to the College, was presenting details and facets of a history to those whose knowledge of the College was bound to be more intimate than mine. I hoped that their delight in the photographs themselves would allow them to forgive me any errors in name, date or circumstance.

The exhibition ran for three months and I returned in October to dismantle the displays and to return the photographs to safe storage. What a pity it was that many former students had not been able to make the journey to Chichester to see the exhibition. What a shame, it seemed, to disperse and 'lose' this assemblage of visual history. Could we not record it in some way? And so, from feelings and questions such as these this book was conceived. The photographs within these pages represent the essence of that exhibition. To complete the book, some additional photographic material has been supplied by **Dave Turner**, a mature student who recently completed an honours degree in Related Arts at the College. His is also chairman of the Chichester Photographic Historic Group. The photographs of the 150th anniversary celebrations were taken by Dr. Tony Barnes, a retired lecturer from the Teaching and Education Studies section.

The text in this book is a simple account of the main themes of College history in each decade since its foundation, and it is accompanied by excerpts from contemporary documents and reports. These contemporary narratives are often fitting partners to the photographs. They present, to a large extent, the smiling face of history – panegyrics and enthusiasms culled from personal memoranda and college magazines. If there were dark sides to the College's history, such as the closure in 1868, or the World War II years, our view is with hindsight, from the vantage point of paradise regained. The College archives themselves remain for those who wish to probe alternative aspects of history.

Heather Warne

Every institution has its own ethos, like any family or any individual. A College is both a family and a parent, an *Alma Mater*. Ethos, as derived from Aristotle's usage, is difficult to define and yet institutions and their members are constantly analysing what makes them special or even unique. Ethos is the "*genius loci*". It incorporates such abstractions as tradition, spiritual climate, style, tone and taste. Bishop Otter College is by no means alone in claiming a particular combination of these characteristics to distinguish itself.

As Head of the College for the last nine years I have often been challenged to state what I, the staff and the students consider is exceptional about it. This I have found singularly difficult to express in words to those who, on the one hand, maintain that the original spirit of the founders can still be detected in its current life and ideals, and to those, on the other, who hold that it is just like any other institution of higher education.

This book is an attempt to let the College itself answer these questions by indicating some of its qualities and eccentricities over a century and a half. It is not a history in the fullest sense but is a character sketch or portrait - perhaps a self portrait.

Trevor Brighton
31st March 1992.

Chapter 1
THE FOUNDATION
1839-1867

... So rapid of late years has been the progress of public opinion in favour of education, so numerous have been the applications for teachers, and so much higher than formerly the standard of qualifications required, that the limited income and resources of the [National] Society are no longer sufficient to supply the increasing demands upon them; - while on the other hand it has been a matter of great regret to the friends of education, that the children in very many poor parishes are left entirely without wholesome instruction for no other reason than that sufficient local funds cannot be raised. [Therefore]... most pressing and important, and that which has been specially recommended by the Archbishop of Canterbury to the Bishops, is the establishment of one or more Diocesan Boards, with a Training Seminary ... in every Diocese.

From William Otter's appeal to the clergy and laity of the Diocese of Chichester for the formation of a Diocesan Board of Education, 29 January 1839.

William Otter, was a Fellow of Jesus College, Cambridge, 1796 - 1804. After serving as a parish priest and school master, he was Principal of King's College, London, 1830 - 1836 and Bishop of Chichester 1836 - 1840. He spent the last four years of his life campaigning throughout the Diocese in the cause of education for all.

His vision for "the key to good social harmony" was that, "every rank shall be made to feel for every other as for itself and all be knit together by the ties of mutual respect, as well of kindness and affection". (Pastoral Addresses, 1836 -1840.)

The day of William Otter's funeral {l} brought together many of the influential persons in the Diocese who were sympathetic to his aims. The occasion was therefore used to hold a meeting in the Cathedral library. This resulted in the formation of a Committee whose express purpose was to establish a Training School dedicated to his memory. It was to be called "Bishop Otter's School for Training Masters", or, later, "Bishop Otter's Training College for School Masters". Thus, on the day of his funeral, were his ideals acknowledged and his new College was effectively founded.

{l} A study of William Otter's life can be read in Otter Memorial Paper No. 6 by Robert Holthy (1990).

The College opened on 11 April 1840 in makeshift premises in St. Martin's Lane. Three students were enrolled. No information survives about the original building. All we know is that it was over a shop, known as Edney's Stores, now demolished. By 1848 forty teachers had been trained there.

Little is known of the activities and achievements of the first College. The first two principals, Rev. Alexander Peters (1842 - 1846) and Rev. Henry Foster (1846 - 1848), have left no record of their work. The third, however, Rev. (later Canon) Matthew Parrington dedicated 20 years to the College from 1848 -1868.

In 1848 Parrington, together with the Bishop, A.T. Gilbert, George Chandler, the Dean of Chichester, H.E. Manning, Archdeacon of Chichester, and J.C. Hare, Archdeacon of Lewes formed a committee "for the purpose of raising fixed and certain funds adequate to (the College's) maintenance".

By 1849 £2,063 had been raised and the necessary land was purchased on which to erect the new College. Principal Parrington immediately engaged Joseph Butler, the Cathedral architect, and sent plans of the proposed building to the Committee of Council on Education at the Privy Council Office, Downing Street. The architect was sent to Oxford to study college architecture there and thus the Tudor-gothic style of Bishop Otter College was conceived.

The architect's design for the new College was to include a chapel, principal's house, cloister, dormitories and classrooms. When opened in 1850 there was no chapel, but in all other respects the College was built as planned. The College probably worshipped in the nearby Church of St. Paul's which Bishop Otter had dedicated immediately after his enthronement in Chichester Cathedral in 1836. The Chapel was added a few years later when sufficient funds had been raised. The College bell, dated 1851, was placed in the cupola over the dormitories. The bell is now presented together with the Chapel bell in the display cabinet in the cloisters.

A. W. VIEW OF BISHOP OTTER'S TRAINING COLLEGE FOR SCHOOL MASTERS AT CHICHESTER.
With a Design for the Proposed Chapel

An out-of-town site beyond the City walls was selected for the new College. By a deed of 10 May, 1849, Bishop Gilbert purchased from James Bennett Freeland, Esq., "... All that piece or parcel containing ... three acres, one rod and fourteen perches, being the north part of the westermost of two fields or closes of meadow land adjoining together ... situated in the Parish of St. Peter the Great ... within the liberties of the City of Chichester. "

"Love Lane" (*opposite*), now called College Lane, still retains today its rural feel. These two views were taken circa 1910 and are reproduced from originals in the possession of Mr Arthur Sivyer of Chichester.

Below: a view of the College in its earliest phase. The chapel was built a few years after 1850 and until 1876 it remained entirely detached.
Cattle continued to graze around the College grounds for at least **another 50 years.**

THE MEN'S COLLEGE AROUND 1860
Matthew Parrington, the Principal, is standing at the centre back wearing a high hat. This is one of only two photographs that survive showing students in the period 1850-1867.

Little documentation survives from the period 1850 - 1867 when male students occupied the College. We are fortunate that in 1899 the College Magazine printed an account of the daily routine of the earlier College.

Study apart, it was a case of "all hands to the pump".

WEEK-DAYS
Rise at Six all the year round.

6.30 to 7.30	Private Study.
7.30	Morning Service in Chapel, except on Wednesdays, Fridays and Saints' Days. (All Saints' Days and Saturdays were half-holidays; students allowed to leave the grounds after dinner, but must return in time for tea at 6. On Saints' Days and during Lent, and other occasions, Evening Service at the Chapel at 8.)
8.00	Lecture.
9.00	Breakfast.
10.00 to 12.00	Lectures, except on Wednesdays, Fridays, and Saints' Days, when Students attended Morning Service in the Cathedral.
12.00	Gardening.
1.00	Dinner.
2.00	Lecture, except for Students attending Central School.
3.30	Recreation. Students allowed to leave the grounds.
5.00	Private Study.
6.00	Tea.
6.30	Lecture.
7.30	Private Study.
9.00	Prayers in Dining Room (Principal.)
10.00	All lights out.

Each Student had to give daily 100 strokes at the pump for water supply of the building, and double the amount on Saturday, the number to be entered in a book kept for the purpose.

SUNDAYS

7.00	The hour for rising.
7.30 to 8.30	Prayers and Bible Reading (Vice-Principal), in Lecture Room.
9.00	Breakfast.
11.00	Morning Service at St. Paul's Parish Church. All Students attended, except one-third, who accompanied the Principal to some neighbouring parish, where he took duty.
1.00	Dinner.
3.00	Afternoon Service at the New Sub-Deanery Church.
6.00	Tea.
7.00	Bible Reading (Vice-Principal.)
8.00	Singing Sacred Music in Dining Room.
9.00	Prayers in Dining Room (Vice-Principal).
10.00	All lights out.

Above: **The west wing of the College formed a residence for the principal and the staff. It is ensigned on the chimney breast with the arms of Bishop Gilbert. A door from the house opened into an unglazed cloister, giving covered passage to the chapel.**

The cedar of Lebanon in the foreground was one of many trees and shrubs planted by Principal Parrington which still enhance the premises today. This photograph dates from circa 1870 at the end of Parrington's era.

Bishop Otter's Training College, Chichester.

———

SCHOOLMASTER'S CERTIFICATE.

We whose names are undersigned, testify that *Alfred Manley* has resided as a Pupil at BISHOP OTTER's TRAINING COLLEGE FOR SCHOOLMASTERS, Chichester, the full time of two years, ending *July* — *1852* and that during that time he conducted himself to the satisfaction of the Committee and Officers:—and we hereby certify THE LORD BISHOP OF THE DIOCESE that we consider him to be fitted, as well by learning and skill in teaching, as by soundness in religious belief and practice, to undertake the management of a Parochial School.

Signed *James Garbett*
Hutchinson
Philip Freeman
Geo. H. Woods

Countersigned *A. T. Chichester*
22 Oct. 1852.

P.C.L. ARCHIVE
N° G. 49

Left: Although few documents relating to the early history of the College survive, strays occasionally turn up as gifts from descendants of former students. The College was fortunate to obtain this Schoolmaster's Certificate in this way.

Donated by Florence Greenfield 1990.

January 28, 1867

*At a meeting of the Committee
… Mr Parrington stated that
after every exertion he could hold
out no prospect that there were
more than four students likely to
come into residence on January
31. It was then resolved: that the
Committee of the training
College, having heard the
statement of Mr Parrington, the
principal of the College, are
compelled to announce to the
subscribers that they can no
longer carry on the Institution.*

*… That the deep felt thanks of
the Committee be offered to Mr
Parrington for his active and
unwearied efforts in carrying on
the College during so many years
of anxiety. . .*

Above: **Angel corbel today, in the
College Library.**

The reopening of the College in 1873 enabled Matthew
Parrington's achievements to live on. Future staff and students were
able to enjoy not only the gardens he created but also the
embellishments of the chapel. The angel corbels (below left) were
carved in situ by the students whom he taught. He and his students
also commenced the wood carving that can be seen in the
photograph on page 37, a tradition that continued for the next fifty
years.

Above: **Interior of the Chapel in 1898, before extension.**

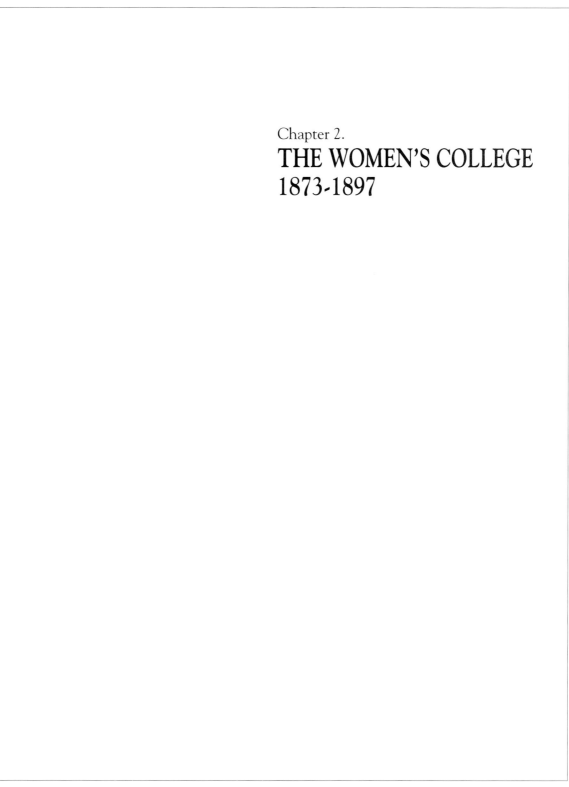

Chapter 2.
THE WOMEN'S COLLEGE
1873-1897

Bishop Otter's Memorial College, we are very glad to learn, is being now prepared for the reception of Lady Students who desire to fit themselves to become certificated teachers in National Schools. The building is at a short distance from Chichester, and is a beautiful structure, with all the requisites for College life, good classrooms, chapel, dormitories, house of residence for the principal, and garden. It was originally designed, and for a time employed as a Training School for schoolmasters, but has for some time been disused, and is now refitted for the use of such ladies as may be anxious to obtain the advantages both of School training and of the art of school management. It is greatly to be hoped that many women of the middle and upper ranks will thankfully avail themselves of this easy and honourable road to a useful self-maintenance. The position of a village School Teacher, with her little house rent-free, and her salary of £50 or £80, may not be a great prize, but it is one which many hundreds of "poor ladies" would find the best of all possible remedies for the "sorrows of gentility", and preferable, for many cogent reasons, to the work of a private governess or companion. Applications for information about Otter College should be made to the lady to whose zeal her countrywomen mainly owe its devotion to its present purpose, Miss Hubbard, of Leonards Lee, Horsham.

Extract from **The Echo***, September 1872*

Bishop Otter College reopened in 1873 as a training college for women, due, principally to the campaign waged towards that aim by Louisa Hubbard.

Bishop Otter's eldest son, William, was a prebendary and then archdeacon of Chichester. He was also the vicar of Cowfold where, as near neighbour to the Hubbard family, he was the vital link that enabled Louisa Hubbard's campaigning energies to be directed towards his father's Jollege. At his death in 1876 his family was torn between making a gift to Cowfold church or endowing the college in his memory. They chose the latter. His daughters went on to become generous benefactresses to the expansion of the College. The Otter family lived in the Cowfold/Lower Beeding area until recent years.

Louisa Hubbard was the daughter of W.E. Hubbard of Leonardslee and later of Selehurst, in Lower Beeding. In 1871 she started campaigning for the acceptance of a role for women as teachers in society and for the re-opening of Bishop Otter's College to receive women students. After the reopening she continued to work for the College on its management committees and as a benefactress.

The College re-opened in 1873 and admitted 26 Students.

Louisa Hubbard died on the 25th November 1906. Apart from her campaign for the College her life's work had been a mission to change public opinion with regard to women working. She argued for the dignity of paid employment. The prejudice of the day was that educated gentle women should not work for money and could not, therefore, have a career or a profession. Her obituary in the Manchester Guardian states that her argument gained ground so that gradually "women took courage to enter upon forms of employment not only more congenial to them than teaching, but often better paid..." Her life's work included the launching of a *Handbook for Women's Work* in 1875 which evolved in the 1880s as *The English Woman 's Year Book*. From 1875 1893 she also published *The Women 's Gazette*, afterwards *Work and Leisure*, which discussed all kinds of women's issues. She was, indeed, an outstanding pioneer in the cause of women's emancipation.

"This College will be opened next January as a *TRAINING SCHOOL*, under Government, on the principles of the Church of England, for Elementary School Mistresses.

The College is intended for Persons who have not been Pupil-Teachers; a preference being given to the Daughters of Clergy and Professional men. About £1,500 will be required to place it in working order, of which one half has been already subscribed. Its scope being distinctly National, and not in any way Diocesan, the Committee appeal for Funds to the country at large. It is hoped that many who are favourable to the undertaking will be glad to offer their aid now that its work is about to commence. Contributions should be sent in before the end of the year.

The attention of intending Students and their Friends is called to the following Regulations:-

1. Candidates for Admission must have completed their Eighteenth Year by January 1st, 1873.
2. They must pass the Examination for Students, held by H.M. Inspectors, in all Training Colleges, in the week commencing December 15th, the expense of which varies from five to ten shillings for board and lodging.
3. Immediate application for Terms of Admission, and for Instructions respecting this Preliminary Examination, should be made to "The Rev. The Chaplain, Otter Memorial College, Chichester."
4. Persons who have passed successfully the Government Examination will, if admitted, be called Government Students, and charged £20 per annum for the two years' residence required by Government; this sum to be paid quarterly in advance.
5. Private Students will also be admitted, when there are vacancies, on payment of £35 for the whole year, or of £20 for six months".

Excerpt from the prospectus of 1872.
(BOC Archives, MS. G/1 fo.22).

Sarah Frances Trevor was the first woman Principal from 1872 until her retirement in 1894. The newly re-opened college was almost entirely in the hands of women, who needed to prove their ability both as managers and as scholars. Fanny Trevor achieved these ends and the college flourished . She died in 1904 and a stained glass window, dedicated to St. Hilda of Whitby, was installed in the chapel in her memory. It is the only stained glass window now surviving within the old chapel.

Elizabeth Davy succeeded Miss Trevor as Principal in 1895. She had been successively a student, a governess and, in 1887, the Vice Principal. She resigned in 1897 due to ill health. The College archives contain no photographs of Miss Davy (unless she is in the 1882 and 1888 year groups - here and on page 16.

One of the first things that Miss Trevor achieved for her students was an improvement in the state of the footpaths in College Lane. "We most certainly wish to do everything in our power to make the road as good and clean as we can and I have directed our men to proceed at once...," stated Frederick Vick, the way warden, in a reply to the College chaplain in 1873.

The Principal with staff and students in 1882.
Fanny Trevor, Principal, seated centrally in bonnett with ribbons.

Above: **The College towards the end of the 19th century.**

Compare the picture on page 7.

The link from the main block to the chapel was completed in 1876, giving the College a library and additional classrooms below and dormitories above. This increased the College's capacity to 40, but 30 was the number of students usually in residence. The new wing was built in limestone in Tudor gothic style, to harmonise with the existing buildings.

A water supply was laid on. The ladies no longer had to take turns at the pump as the men had done. In all other respects, however, facilities were primitive. The dormitories consisted of a long central aisle with curtained cubicles on either side, affectionately referred to as 'cubes' by the students.

Below: **A student's 'cube' circa 1915 (Dorothy Earl's archive).**

Photograph given by I.M. Robertson.

In the Men's College 1840-1867 and in the Women's College 1873-1900 many of the students had come in from schools where their education had been rather basic, but where their ability had given them the chance to become pupil teachers. From 1873, alongside the pupil teachers were young ladies from a sheltered middle class background who had usually been educated privately at home. Neither group was broadly educated by modern standards. In the face of some opposition from the educationists of the time, Miss Trevor encouraged the entry of the latter group and the "pupil teachers" were gradually phased out.

However, this "Lesson in Criticism," (above) dates from around 1897 and it looks as though many of the class members were under 18 and that they were therefore pupil teachers.

Above: **At least one of the early teaching staff at the College achieved fame beyond its walls. Charlotte Mason became senior governess in 1873 (the full complement of resident staff then being Principal, senior and junior governesses). In 1877 she moved on to Bradford where she founded the Parents' Educational Union, later to become the P.N.E.U. In 1892 she founded the Charlotte Mason College at Ambleside, which still survives. She was its first Principal from its foundation until her death in 1923. Her obituary in the 'Times' credited her with being more influential in education than anyone in her time. A proposal for a Charlotte Mason memorial in Bishop Otter College was mooted in council in 1961, but was not taken up.**

Photograph: (taken in 1864) from the Story of Charlotte Mason by Essex Cholmondeley.

The curriculum from 1873 to 1897 was classified under two headings A. secular knowledge and B. religious knowledge. There were few subject specialists on the staff apart from the music teacher and the chaplain. From the annual reports, however, we can detect that mathematics, english, history and geography were taught, as well as geometry, freehand and perspective drawing and botany. For the last, it was remarked in 1889 that results were good because students had special lessons from a "science master." Craft was also taught, meaning needle-craft as the photograph above illustrates (circa 1898). "Industrial work" was another craft subject, possibly handicrafts.

In 1886 Principal Fanny Trevor stated that the students found recreation in "lawn tennis and walks". Two hours in the middle of the day were allocated for walks in the country. Moreover, "they frequently dance of an evening".

Below: **We see them exercising with Indian clubs circa 1895.**

Above: **1st year students 1888.**

These two photographs, together with the group shown on p. 12 above are the only year groups that survive from Fanny Trevor's College.

The magnificent Bernese mountain dog probably belonged to Miss Trevor.

Below: **2nd year students 1888.**

Chapter 3.
EXPANSION
1897-1919

Below: **Staff and students, 1906-1908.**

The Rev. Edwin Hammonds was Principal from July 1897 until retirement in 1919, a "golden era" of growth and stability for the College. He rapidly achieved major improvements in equipment, facilities and accommodation, bringing the number of resident students from 40 in 1897 to 100 by 1905. His wife provided practical support in the College and their daughter went to Oxford University and returned here to teach.

Right: **He is pictured with his wife.**

Their only son was killed in the First World War. Mrs Hammonds died in 1931 and he himself in 1933. Wall plaques were erected in his and his son's memory in the old chapel. They are now on display in the cloisters.

The first 8 years of Hammonds' principalship were devoted to the enlargement of the College premises and the improvement of facilities in order to provide the students with the most up-to-date education. He actively sought donations from existing and new subscribers. Foremost among the new friends of the College was Julia Henty of Oaklands House (which lies opposite the College in College Lane). She made a loan of £2,000 towards the cost of new building. Finally, on 13 September 1901, the moneys were counted and, including £150 from a forthcoming fund-raising bazaar, were found to be sufficient. It was resolved "...that the Enlargement Committee hereby authorise the Architect to make the necessary arrangements for carrying out the whole of the work ... at the contract price of £3,560".

Below: **Aerial photograph, taken in 1923, shows the new wings on the east side of college (right side of photograph). A three-storey wing north of, and parallel with, the Chapel was officially opened in 1902. A further wing returned south and was opened in 1905. Note the amount of ivy covering the buildings. The garden in the middle came to be known as "Chapel Quad". The architect of the new wings was Gordon Hills and the builder was J.O. Holt.**

Above: **A view of the new gas-lit science room taken circa 1905.**

Among the facilities provided by the new wings were a properly equipped science laboratory and a new hall. New dormitories were located on the top and second floors.

By a resolution passed in College Council on 3 June 1901 the new dormitories were to be called Randall, Henty, Burgon and Trevor, after benefactors and the former Principal. The two old dormitories in the existing buildings were to be called Richmond and Chichester, after the Duke of Richmond and the Bishop.

Left: South Side of the new wing. **Photograph taken in 1970 by College photographer Derrick Kyte of the Media Services section.**

The new premises were dedicated by the Archbishop of Canterbury on 16 April 1901. The occasion was recorded photographically below

His words were recorded as follows:

He had come that afternoon to discharge a very pleasant duty. It was to declare that those buildings were now open and ready for use, and they would forth with be applied to the purpose for which they were erected. They were dedicated in a very real sense to the service of God, because it was one of the most important services they could render to Him to provide for the right education for the children of this country. (Annual Report 1900 - 1901)

Above: **The Recreation Room; 1901**

A large sitting room, beautifully furnished, is used entirely for recreation purposes and is fitted up for indoor games: it has a library of its own.
(Principal Hammonds)

Rooms in the old block which were formerly used for teaching were now released for other purposes. The new "Sitting Room" is the same location as the former "Junior Classroom", now (1992) downstairs in the library.

Below; **The dedication ceremony 1901.**

The College circa 1900.
Above: Principal Hammonds is seated centrally.
This is one of the earliest year groups taken during Hammonds's
principalship in the College Archives.

Right: The library "circa 1901", in enlarged accommodation following the
opening of the new wing. In 1899 there was an "adequate" library
containing 320 books, for which new additions were chosen "with great
discretion". (Council minutes). After 1900 a purchasing policy was
enthusiastically followed, financed by keeping pigs in the College grounds.
The following excerpt from the College Magazine (1900) serves to
illustrate the point:

*The College pigs are having a very dull time; they had not finished
paying for the encyclopaedia when the Century Dictionary arrived. Deep
sighs and groans were heard from the sty for they knew that many, many
fat pigs must live and die ere the debt be paid.*

The Report of Her Majesty's Inspector for Education in 1901 -
1902 was enthusiastic about the quality of the College's library and
described it as

*A Library with carefully selected books of reference and handsomely
fitted up ... is pronounced by the inspectorate to be one of the finest in the
kingdom. The daily papers and educational periodicals are also to be
found here.*

Drama played an important part in the early extra-curriculum of the College. After 1901 the new wing provided a roomy hall for performances, but events were still frequently staged in the grounds.

Below: **The cast from *A Midsummer Night's Dream,* 1906.**

Left: **Contemporary account in the College Magazine.**

THE Annual Prize Distribution took place on Saturday, June 27th, and was attended by a large gathering of members of the Council, residents of Chichester and neighbourhood and friends of the Students.

The Lord Bishop of Chichester presided and also distributed the prizes to the Students. After the distribution, he gave an interesting address, dealing specially with the great importance of the work of a Teacher.

At various intervals during the proceedings, some delightful Part-songs were rendered by the Students, under the direction of Mr. Crowe.

After tea, in the grounds, an excellent representation of " A Midsummer Night's Dream," (Act v.) was given by the Junior Students under the management of Miss Hammonds.

" A MIDSUMMER NIGHT'S DREAM."
Act V.

(Theseus, Duke of Athens, celebrates his Wedding with Hippolyta, Queen of the Amazons, by hearing the play of " Pyramus and Thisbe," carefully rehearsed for the occasion by certain " rude mechanicals " among his subjects. At the conclusion of the festivities, Oberon and Titania and their train appear to bless the Palace and its inhabitants. Puck speaks an apology for the players).

CHARACTERS.

Theseus	..	M. Long	..	Prologue	..	E. Moore.
Hippolyta	..	E. Parrington		Thisbe	..	G. Blunn.
Lysander	..	M. Rookwood		Wall	..	K. King.
Demetrius	..	E. Bonner	..	Moonshine	..	E. Comper
Helena	..	H. Price	..	Lion	..	A. Burgess.
Hermia	..	A. Sare	..	Pyramus	.	A. Collins.
Philostrate	..	E. Mortimer				

Oberon	..	G. Mitchell.
Titania	..	F. Jones.
Puck	..	M. Barnett.

Courtiers.	Attendants.	Fairies.

Incidental Music by Mendelssohn, rendered by an Orchestra and the Senior Students.

Stage Manager	..	Miss Hammonds
Musical Conductor	..	Mr. F. J. W. Crowe.

Below: **Principal characters from *Julius Caesar,* 1903.**

23

Bishop Otter's College, Chichester

y weather here yesterday, so Mary, bonnie
—alid to Goodwood Park in the bath cha—
—b.t. me know how you are. won't
to both from Rhoda

Bishop Otter College, Chichester.

SUNDAY ARRANGEMENTS.

1. There will be a Celebration of Holy Communion every Sunday at 8 a.m. On the second Sunday of each month it is hoped that all students will be present at this Service.
2. With the exception of the second, and the last Sunday in each month all students are expected to attend the Cathedral Service at 10.30 a.m., and should be in their seats not later than 10.25 a.m., entering by the South Door only ; they should sit as far forward as possible. The Chapel Bell will be rung at 10 a.m., for five minutes, by which time all students should have left the College grounds. Students may not leave the Cathedral till after the Prayer for the Church Militant.
3. Choral Evensong in the College Chapel at 7 p.m.
4. **Sunday is not recognized as a day for receiving, or paying visits.**

THE MONTHLY EXEAT.

1. Students will be allowed to spend the last week-end in the month with their friends whenever possible ; the permission will extend from Saturday after dinner till Monday 1 p.m.
2. Students may spend the time at their own homes, or with their friends, subject to the consent of their parents and the College Authorities.
3. Students spending the holiday at College are subject to the ordinary rules, except that on Sunday they are free to go to any Church in the neighbourhood, provided they return at the usual times for meals, unless special permission is obtained for going out to tea. The times of roll-call will be announced. On Monday mornings students are free to go out till dinner-time.
4. A special time-table of work will be arranged for Monday afternoons.

RECREATION.

1. Each afternoon from 2 till 4.30 is, as a rule, free for recreation, and should not, unless under very exceptional circumstances, be used for other purposes. From a health point of view it is necessary that as much *outdoor* exercise as possible be taken every day. Long expeditions, exceeding a total of 8 miles walking, or 20 cycling, must not be taken without the special permission of the Lady Superintendent.
2. Students are not allowed to go out walking, or cycling alone ; and may not go into Chichester, without special permission, on more than two days a week.
3. Permission must be obtained from the Lady Superintendent before paying visits in Chichester and the neighbourhood, or before introducing visitors into the College.
4. Bathing, boating, and driving, or travelling by train, are not allowed without special permission.

ABSENCE FROM COLLEGE.

Permission must first be obtained **from the Principal** for any unavoidable absence from the College, and in the case of illness, a medical certificate must always be sent. Details of the illness should at the same time be sent to the Lady Superintendent.

EDWIN HAMMONDS, *Principal.*

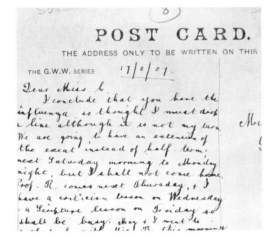

POST CARD.

THE ADDRESS ONLY TO BE WRITTEN ON THIS

THE G.W.W. SERIES 17/2/07

Dear Miss C.
I conclude that you have the
influenza so thought I must drop
a line although it is not my turn
We are going to have an extension of
the exeat instead of half term
next Saturday morning to Monday
night, but I shall not come home.
Prof. R. comes next Thursday, + I
have a criticism lesson on Wednesday
a Scripture lesson on Friday so
shall be busy. May + I went to

Postcards from Student "Rhoda" to Miss Colbourne in 1907 give an insight into College life (*left*), as do the "Rules" in 1911 (among Maud Godwin's archives). Rhoda's second postcard refers to the "exeat" ["She may go out"] and this is amplified in the Rules (*above*).

Lecture Hall, Bishop Otters' College, Chichester
This is where we have our dances, + drill.

Left: Rhoda's postcard shows the new hall which Principal Hammonds described in 1901 as *... such a boon to us. Criticism lessons, Drill, Music, Art Classes, Science demonstrations, Entertainments of all kinds dancing, and no heavy desks to move out of the way - what visions the mere thought of such a room seems to bring!* (College Magazine).

Bognor, Bosham, Arundel, Selsey and Goodwood are among the most favoured places, all being within easy distance of the College
(*College Magazine 1900*).

In 1900 a cycle run to London was attempted by two students but abandoned at Redhill due to punctures.

Recreation circa 1900

Special attention is being given to the recreation of the Students. The College time table has been so arranged that every afternoon is free for cycling, walks, tennis etc.. A cycling club has been formed. Those students who had machines were allowed to bring them, and through subscriptions of the staff and students, a bicycle has already become the property of the club.
(*College Magazine 1900*).

Above: **The Cyling Club outside the College gates 1899** ⋅

Postcards from Student "Rhoda" to Miss Colbourne in 1907 give an insight into College life (*left*), as do the "Rules" in 1911 (among Maud Godwin's archives). Rhoda's second postcard refers to the "exeat" ["She may go out"] and this is amplified in the Rules (*above*).

In the early 1900s extra-curricular activities of all kinds were encouraged. As well as cycling there was hockey, tennis and folk dancing. The last was encouraged by H.M.I. Mr Burrows, who was an enthusiast. Indoors there were theatricals and dances, including fancy dress, as well as guest lectures, concerts, lantern shows and recitations. By 1907 a Literary Society, a Choral Society and a Physical Recreation Society had appeared, with a Debating Society and a Sketching Club hard on their heels.

Above: **Folk dancing on the lawn, 1905.**

Tennis was popular. The court shown below was "the most popular one", there being a less favoured grass court on the north of the building together with an asphalt one given by Miss Trevor. The first recorded match was in 1899 on a Saturday in June, an occasion proving... *to be all that one could wish, and the naturally pretty grounds presented a very attractive scene, with the spectators seated in groups on the spacious lawn.... Amidst great excitement the winning stroke was played by Miss K. M. Holman, Miss M. O. Holman carrying off the second prize. This was presented by Mr. Burrows who made a short speech in which he expressed his pleasure at being able to witness so pleasing a spectacle.*
(*College Magazine 1899*)

Two formidable arrays

The College Council, 1908.

3 standing in doorway: Rev J.C.B. Fletcher, J.A. Penfold Wyatt Esq., P.T. Mackeson Esq.;

Back row standing: Col. Hilyard, Rev. Dr. Codrington, W.L. Gibbings, Esq., Canon Deane, G.E. Maltby Esq., Rev. W.F. Shaw, Chancellor Davy.

Front row seated: Canon Masters, Mrs Masters, Ven. Archdeacon of Chichester, Rt. Rev. Ernest R. Wilberforce, Bishop of Chichester, Rev. E. Hammonds, Mrs. Upcott.

Edwin Hammonds's years at Bishop Otter College were those of a father - a father to his own daughter, who studied here, and to his extended family of daughters. We are fortunate that students' snapshots have captured some of their serene moments of relaxation in the grounds. A few years hence World War I was to replace their frills and furbelows with a more purposeful attire that suited the working woman far better than stiff Edwardian styles.

Right: **Lucy Mason (later Mills).**

Below: **Lucy Mason's friends relaxing with Principal Hammonds.**
(sepia snapshot, 1910).

Above: **Dorothy Earl's friends Maud, Margaret and Emma.**
(sepia snapshot., 1913.)

Below: **Daisy Read and friends as
V.A.D. girls, 1918.**
(Daisy seated centre front).

In the First World War

In the front garden near the Cloisters, Miss Boaler is growing gargantuan shallots and Miss Griffiths monster lettuces ....

.... The students' gardens at the back are packed with vegetable seeds, and in the new rose garden, alongside the steps down to the hockey field, they have prepared beds of carrots and celery.

.... it is a question of surmise whether the hockey field may not soon be displaced by potatoes.
College Magazine 1918

Below: **The lawn provided its usual serene setting for events. The occasion recorded here was a Guild Reunion, 3 June 1916. "The atmosphere of the day was somewhat disturbed by news of a great naval battle in the North Sea... but in spite of this, everyone managed to spend a very enjoyable day".**
The photograph gives a rare glimpse of the College servants.

Staff and senior students, 1916.

Apart from its incentive for growing vegetables and giving concerts and entertainments in aid of nursing funds, the First World War did little to interrupt the smooth flow of College routine.

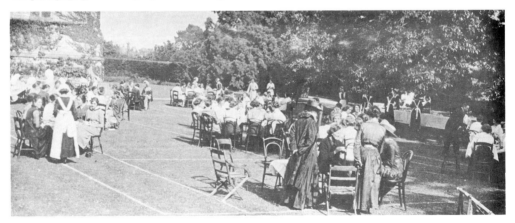

Chapter 4.
THE CHAPEL

Chapel and Main College Wing, circa 1873.

The chapel was designed in 1849 at the same time as the original College buildings, but was erected a few years later as soon as enough money could be raised. The view (*left*) shows it still detached from the main buildings.

The bell cote has since (?in 1933) been removed. The vestibule is integral with the main buildings and is part of the present library.

In 1929 the original bell was found to be cracked and was replaced, at a cost of £30, by a new bell cast by Messrs. Gillett and Johnston of Croydon. It was transferred to a campanile south of the new chapel and is now preserved in the cloisters.

Above: **Dedication day, 15 November, 1902.**

It would seem, at first glance, that we are looking at the same interior (above) as that in 1898, shown on page 8. Instead we are seeing the eastern extension in which the same window, mullions and tracery have been replaced and embellished with stained glass. New carved angel corbels have been continued into the extension to provide continuity with the decorative scheme devised by Matthew Parrington in the 1850s.

In 1897 Principal Hammonds increased the number of students in college and it became difficult to accommodate everyone in the chapel. The chaplain, Rev. J Fraser, offered a temporary solution by dismantling the organ, which was at the east end of the nave, and re-assembling it at the west end: but further help was at hand. Sufficient subscriptions came in during the 1899 - 1900 building programme to enable an extension of the chapel eastwards. At the same time a new east window was inserted at a cost of £150. The well-known Sussex glass - painter C. E. Kempe was commissioned for the work and he created a crucifixion scene in the centre light with St. Mary the Virgin and St. John in devotional postures in the side lights. It was installed in December 1900, celebrating the 50th year of the College's history. Further stained glass was added a few years later to fill the lower parts of the lights. A carved reredos was installed on 9 October 1904 and dedicated by the Bishop of Chichester (see page 34). Between 1904 and 1910 three more windows were installed, one of them in the memory of Principal Fanny Trevor to commemorate her 30 years service. Some of these have since been installed in the cloisters.

Chichester Diocesan Gazette.

Dedication of the Enlarged Chapel of Bishop Otter College.

On Saturday, November 8th, a Special Service was held at the BISHOP OTTER COLLEGE, Chichester, at which the enlarged chapel was dedicated by the LORD BISHOP.

In recent years the work of the College has greatly increased; and with the large number of students now undergoing training there, the authorities have long felt the need of adding to the limited accommodation provided by the Chapel. A scheme of enlargement by setting back the eastern wall a distance of about 30ft., and adding a new portion to that end of the building, was found practicable; and the work has recently been completed by Mr. J. O. Holt from designs prepared by Mr. Gordon P. Hills. The enlargement will afford about a third more accommodation than that formerly provided, and will, it is believed, serve the purposes of the College for many years to come. The total length of the enlarged Chapel is 65ft.

9in., of which 10ft. 4in. forms an ante-chapel. The stalls are retained; and there are 12 rows of seats for the students, so as to accommodate 96 students, servants, and visitors, as well as the staff in the existing stalls. A space of 15 feet is assigned to the altar approach and sanctuary, and a door has been placed in the north wall leading to that space. The east end window, designed by Mr. Kempe, is replaced 18 inches higher than formerly, the £150 required for the stained glass being given as a thanksgiving by the staff and students of the past 30 years. The cost of the scheme was about £900, for which Mrs. Douglas Henty, and Chancellor Davey (who each contributed a donation of £100), and Prebendary Fraser, kindly gave a personal guarantee for £600. In addition to the handsome donations mentioned, smaller sums have since been collected to the amount of £100, and at the special Service on Saturday the offertory brought in £16 17s.

The Chapel was most beautifully decorated for Saturday's Service, this work having been undertaken by Miss Gee and Miss Beatty, assisted by the students. Among those present at the service, in addition to Bishop Wilberforce, were the Dean, Canon Masters (who carried the pastoral staff), Chancellor Davey, Prebendaries Fraser and Codrington, Rev. E. Hammonds (Principal of the College), the Mayor (Councillor Peyton Mackeson), Sir Evan Nepean, Major-General Parry, Mr. J. W. Turing, Mrs. Wilberforce, Mrs. Hannah, Mrs. Douglas Henty, and the Hon. Albertine Grosvenor, with the staff and students of the College. The Dean read the Lesson; and the Lord Bishop, having previously read the Prayers of Dedication, delivered a short Address from the words "So the King and all the Children of Israel dedicated the House of the Lord" (1 Kings, viii. 63). During the Service the Hymns, "The Church's one Foundation," "Come, Holy Ghost, our souls inspire," "Christ is our Corner Stone," and "Now thank we all our God," together with the Anthem, "O praise the Lord," were sung; and Miss Westaway, who was at the organ, was responsible for the excellent musical arrangements.

Top Right: **Account of the enlargement and dedication, 15 November 1902.**

Above top: The organ is seen in its position at the west end of the chapel. It had been removed from the chancel in 1897 in order to make more room for seating and it remained at the west end throughout the life of the chapel.

Above: A view taken circa 1970 by College photographer Derrick Kyte showing the extended length of the chapel.

Above: **Chapel Interior 1961.**

Photograph taken just before the chapel was converted to the College library, showing the wood panelling, stained glass windows on the south side, and poppy heads carved by Miss Westaway.

Below: **The Reredos, 1903.**

Designed by Henry Weaver of Hereford. This was replaced, sometime after the Second World War, by a retable painted by Marguerite Thompson and given by Bishop George Bell.

Embellishments to the chapel were paid for by subscriptions and donations from friends, students and ex-students of the College. Between 1902 and 1914 the walls were entirely clad with carved oak panelling to a design by Henry Weaver of Hereford. Six panels a year were all that could be afforded. It appears that the poppy heads on the pew ends were carved in College. Miss Westaway was named as one of the carvers (thus carrying on Principal Parrington's example).

The stained glass windows from the Kempe and Towers studio were added in 1904 (St. Hilda Abatissa, dedicated to the memory of Principal Trevor), in 1907 (St. Faith the martyr) in 1908 (St. Catherine – completing a double window with St. Faith) and in 1913 two more windows on the south side of Chapel (Sts. Margaret of Scotland, Cecilia, Agnes and Helena).

In 1903 a reredos was designed by Henry Weaver, its panels filled with oil paintings designed and executed by Miss Downes, the whole theme conceived by members of the College Guild of former students. It was installed in chapel in October 1904. Finally, as the last of the pre-war embellishments, a carved oak altar rail was installed in 1914.

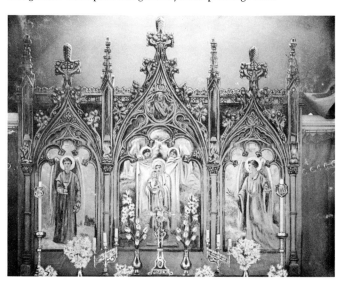

Chapel orderlies 1910.
Principal Hammonds is seated
centrally with Miss Hogg on his
left and Miss Westaway on his
right. The others are students
whose names are now lost to us.

The everyday management and care of the chapel was committed to the chapel orderlies or monitresses, a team of staff and students. *The posts of chapel monitresses are appreciated as a much coveted privilege by the second year students, so that it is difficult to make selection from the eager volunteers. . . ,* reported the Principal in 1909.

The College chapel was never introspective and the orderlies were kept busy in a variety of ways. It was opened for local Sunday school services, for confirmations and for special services with visiting preachers. The Bishop was a frequent visitor. The offertory was dedicated to numerous causes outside the College walls including local hospitals, missionary work in Africa and Church of England charities.

Chapel orderlies 1923.
An informal snapshot taken by
student Elaine Brogatski (alias
Brogate), herself a chapel orderly.
Miss Westaway is on the far
right. (In 1936, after 40 years on
the staff, Miss Westaway became
acting Principal for one term).

Photographed by Dave Turner.

Above Top: **Details of the wood panelling - the green man and a chimera -** installed in the chapel between 1902 and 1914. Unlike the angel corbels, many of which are now damaged, and the stained glass, almost all of which was removed, the wood panelling remains today in the old chapel. *(College Library).*

Above: **A service in 1953 shows** the wood panelling and the pew ends, many of which were carved by Miss Westaway (see preceding page for her photograph.)

Chapel Staff and Orderlies 1924
Back row: **Edith Town, Mary
Warren, Mary Wade, Margery
Hammond, Mary Scovell, Elaine
Brogatski (Brogate).**

Front row: **Nora Potter, Miss
Griffiths (Matron), Florence
Johnson, Principal, Miss
Westaway, Vice-President
(History Specialist), Jesse (née
Goodall) Cooper, head orderly.**

*Photograph from Elaine Brogatski's
archives.*

Florence Johnson (Principal 1919 - 1930) continued to encourage gifts and donations towards the chapel. The chapel vestibule was enriched by the addition of 2 stained glass windows, the first depicting St.Francis of Assisi, (right) installed in 1928; the second, depicting St Richard of Chichester, (left) was installed in 1930, a gift from the students of 1928 - 1930. These two male saints were created by the glass-painter Margaret Roper. The dedication of the St. Francis window was marked by a performance by the 1925-1927 students of *The Little Plays of St. Francis.*

Photographed by Dave Turner.

Chapel Orderlies' Reunion 1927.
Elaine Brogatski and her friends
(years 1922- 1924). Elaine
herself is seated third from the
right.
Reproduced from a sepia snapshot.

Letter of Florence Johnson to the
Old Students 1928.

May 28th

My dear Old Student

A fortnight ago Nora Cripps sent me a cheque from your year, and I am writing to say how gratefully the College accepts this generous token of your affection. I am instructed to get a stained-glass window with a figure of St. Francis for the Chapel porch if the money will run to it; and, failing this, pictures for the Dining Hall, including a picture of St. Francis. It will be a real delight to me to do this, and I will let you know the results of my efforts as soon as I am able.

Your Year needs no single memorial in this College: it will be remembered for its vitality and friendliness and for its keen zest in work and play. To the Staff and myself it will always be the "Franciscan" Year. None the less the College will treasure a special reminder of you all.

I am writing to say "thank you" to every member of the Year; I do not know which of you have contributed to your gift, and that does not matter. It is quite impossible for everyone to give during the first year of settling down to work, and I know that you are all associated with it by your goodwill and affection.

My best wishes to you all.

Yours affectionately

Florence Johnson

Above: **Cast of** *The Little Plays of St. Francis* **1928.**
(Daphne Edwards's Archive)

Chapel orderlies 1930-31.
Back row, standing:
C. Owen, M. Bush, M. Berry, C. Dunlop, E. Brian, K. Archard, M. King.
Seated on chairs:
Elsie Bazeley, Principal, B Bromage, Father Pass, R. Eustan, Miss Stella Westaway.
Seated on grass:
G. Stoke, H. Fox.

The College has no photographs of the chapel in the 1940s. During the war years the R. A . F. were quartered on the College campus and they appear to have welcomed the chapel's presence. On its return to Chichester, Bishop Otter College directed its surplus cash to expansion; artistic impulses were satisfied by the new policy of buying original paintings for the walls of lecture rooms and common rooms. A trickle of donations for the chapel continued, but the hey day of the old chapel as a centre for artistic energy was over.

The chapel continued, however, as a focus for the spiritual life of the College and as a medium between the students and the needs of the community.

In 1952-3 a new organ was installed, built by Messrs Walker, and dedicated on 15 January 1953.

Left: **Ringing the chapel bell, 1953.**

Altar frontals: **White, Red, green (blue)** -(bought with gifts from friends and chapel funds and grant from the College Council.)

Lentern (linen) with lectern cover, and riddled curtains.

Violet: altered by Miss Chesters (c. orderlies 1928-9).

Altar with stone top from Lewes Priory (gift of Miss Johnson).

Altar Rails

3 prie-dieux

Flower stand

Seats in santuary with cushions (6): gift of students and Miss Munroe, 1928.

Small credence table (lent from College furniture in Miss Murray's flat).

Music chest (made by K. Scott) from chapel fund.

1 white rug

Carpet runners at altar rail

Choir chairs

Choir stalls

3 pews with carved ends (done by Miss Westaway).

12 large hassocks/kneelers} covers woven in College by students and staff.

Carved cupboards in ante chapel

2 boards with prayer of St. Francis, St. Richard} students.

1 notice board (too hard).

Left: **Excerpt from the inventory of Chapel furnishings, 1961.**

Centre: **The choir. 1953.**

It is impossible to meet all the requests for help at Charity fairs, Church bazaars, etc, but the choir sang again at Christmas at the Rotary Club Tree of Goodwill and at the service in the Cathedral, at which offerings are made for the work of moral welfare in the diocese: a performance of national dances was also given at the St Pancras Community Fair. The list of Sunday Schools at which students help has been lengthened by the addition of a School newly started at the Barracks. Report, 1951.

The College choir was robed for the first time and affiliated to the Royal School of Church Music in 1947.

The choir is pictured here at the chapel vestibule door with chaplain Canon Eperson standing centrally at the back.

Photograph donated by Mrs. J Fernee (née Chapman) who is third from the right in the back row.

The Choir, 1955.

In 1961 a new chapel was nearing completion and the old chapel was about to be converted for use as part of the College library. An inventory of fixtures and fittings was made, some of which found their way to the new chapel. A questionnaire was taken as to what ought to happen to the stained glass windows. Student opinion was overwhelmingly in favour of keeping them in place. The windows were removed, since when some were retrieved from beneath the chapel floor by the present Head of College, Dr. Trevor Brighton, and installed in the cloisters.

The Old Chapel, 1962.
Looking east.

Looking west.

Chapter 5.
THE PRACTICE SCHOOL
1873-1921

Bishop Otter's Memorial College, Chichester

FOR TRAINING LADIES AS ELEMENTARY SCHOOL MISTRESSES.

The Practising SCHOOL in connection with this College will be opened by THE LORD BISHOP OF CHICHESTER, on Monday, April 13th, when the pleasure of your Company and that of your friends is requested.

An Answer addressed to the Lady Principal will oblige.

Service in the Chapel	2.30 p.m.
Opening of the School	3.00 p.m.
Tea at the College	4.00 p.m.
Amateur Concert in the Schoolroom	7.30 p.m.

The Treasurer of the College presents to the Subscribers an Abstract of Accounts for the past year, and begs to remind them that Subscriptions for 1874 are now due.

The sum of £200 is still required to complete the Fittings, & c., of the Model School.

With the re-opening of the College in 1873, it was decided to provide a school on the site in which the students could practice their teaching. The school opened in 1874 with a headmistress and a small staff. It recruited girls and infants from the trading and lower middle classes, each pupil paying 6d. to 8d. a week. In 1876 it received a grant from the National Society for Promoting the Education of the Poor, towards building costs.

In 1886 Principal Fanny Trevor complained that, being ¾ mile from town it was difficult to attract pupils and "in wet weather it is particularly difficult to get the infants to attend". Nevertheless there were 80-90 girls and 20-30 infants in the school. In 1889-90 a small extra classroom was opened for infants.

The school was regarded by College staff as a most useful department of the College, as "furnishing students with experience in the Management of a School and in the practice of teaching" (Report 1875). It was run by a Miss Hodgson, assisted by Miss Adames. In 1881 the school was credited with "very good" standards in literature, domestic economy, grammar and needlework, but geography was only "fair" and mathematics failed to get a mention.

Left: The wing at the west entrance of 'Reception' today was an art block in the early 1900s and by 1910 a 'sick bay'. It seems likely that this was the original Practice School block, made redundant by 1900 following the purchase of new land to the north.

Opposite page: Invitation to the opening ceremony in 1874 and tactful reminder re. subs.

A class in 1898:
Photographed in their play area, north of the present Senior Common Room.

The work of the school has been admirably carried on by the new headmistress (Miss Eastham), and her staff and assistants, and has given great satisfaction to Her Majesty's Inspectors. Annual Report of 1897-8.

The same class in costume, 1898:

The children were occasionally allowed to take part in plays and other costume events in the main College. Unfortunately this one was too early to be recorded in the College Magazines which commenced in 1899.

The two photographs above were lent to the College by Mrs Chitty in response to an appeal in the local newspapers in December 1989 for any memories and mementos of the Practice School. They are the only known photographic record of the School before 1900.

Above: **The Practice School buildings (as completed in 1900) in 1982.**
They lie on the north of the College buildings and present the first aspect
of the College to the majority of visitors who come by car. They are now
offices.

Bishop Otter's College,

CHICHESTER.

PRACTISING SCHOOL BUILDING FUND.

REPORT.

THE new Practising School in connection with the College
was formally opened by THE LORD BISHOP OF CHI-
CHESTER, on April 13th, 1874, and has continued to make
satisfactory progress, both as regards the numbers and
attainments of the Scholars; whilst it has also afforded the
Students an opportunity of making themselves familiar with
the practical duties of their future profession.

In consequence of the sudden death of the Contractor,
an unavoidable delay has occurred in closing the Building
Account; but this has now been done, and the Committee
beg to submit to the Subscribers the subjoined Financial
Statement, with their sincere thanks for the contributions
so kindly and liberally entrusted to their care.

They feel sure that the Subscribers will welcome the
fact that the success of the College, to which they have
liberally contributed, is so fully assured that it already
needs enlargement. The applications for admission are
numerous, and the staff of Teachers needed for the present
Students would suffice for double their number. An increase
in the number accommodated would therefore diminish the
average working expenses per head, and be a matter of wise
economy. The Committee avail themselves of this opportunity of laying the matter before the Subscribers, in the
hope of engaging their sympathy and further support in
this work of extension, which has become necessary for the
full efficiency of the College.

Donations to "Bishop Otter's College Enlargement
Fund" may be paid to the Chaplain, The Rev. R.
'ESPINASSE, Westhampnett Vicarage, Chichester, or to
the Treasurer, R. DENDY, Esq., the Bank, Chichester, or
to the Account of the College, at Messrs. COUTTS & Co.'s,
London.

The opening of the School
in 1874 marked the beginning
of a campaign for further funds
and improvements. The
school's successes were praised
in the College's annual reports
but in 1896 the accom-
modation was condemned by
H.M. Inspectors as inadequate.
By November of the same year
£465 was raised and one acre of
land, to the north of the
college premises, was purchased
from West Sussex County
Council. The total cost of
buying the land, building and
equipping the school was
around £1,000. By 1900
Principal Hammonds was able
to boast that "...handsome
additions have been made to
the Practising Schools which
have been put into a thorough
state of efficiency".

The teaching staff was
raised to three to enable the
head mistress to devote more
time to training the College
students. The H.M.I. Report
now regarded it as "a model
School".

The Boer War caused some
difficulty. There was a "serious
falling off of numbers ...chiefly
by the loss of children from the
Barracks".

Above: **The school children demonstrate their artistry to teacher and photographer, 1907.**
In 1907 Miss Eastham retired "after ten years of faithful and successful work" [College Report] and was replaced by Miss Chignell, while a Miss Cutton was in charge of infants.
Unfortunately it is not known which teacher is shown in photograph.

Above: The School uniform; circa 1906.

Top right: Empire Day 1906-7
Empire day 1906-7 was marked by a gathering of staff, students and servants of the College and the teachers and students of the Practising schools in front of the College buildings. The Principal gave an address and the Union Jack was hoisted for the fist time, to strains of God Save the Queen.
College Magazine

Above, and top and centre right: **Three photographs showing different aspects of the Practice School's activities were lent to the College by Mrs Sampson of Bognor as a result of a newspaper appeal December 1989.**

Centre: School outing to Goodwood.

Right: An undated photograph showing the school children circa 1910.

After tea the company arranged themselves on the terrace and the children of the College Practising School proceeded to play their part in entertaining the audience. The piece was a short version of the familiar story of "The Pied Piper of Hamelin." Miss Chignell, the head mistress, had long been busy with the choruses, and many were the rehearsals on the playground. Mrs. Hammonds had drawn up the little pageant, arranged the dresses, and costumed some very magnificent ladies, who looked so sedate and imposing it was difficult to believe that they were only "Standard VII." in Tudor bravery. The Town Council in red and black had a dignified Academical appearance round the Burgomaster in a purple furred robe and velvet cap, while the Pied Piper in his traditional red and yellow, played his part excellently. A burst of applause greeted the dramatic moment when the little infants in their quaint German dresses detached themselves from the crowd and set off at a trot after the revengeful piper and his magic music, and were soon lost in the shrubbery. The appearance of the little townsfolk of Hamelin in their bright, peasant costumes, was most picturesque, and they acted their parts with such evident enjoyment and so much natural action that the performance was hailed as a great success and gave everybody pleasure, which was fully shared by those who had promoted and arranged it.

Above left: **The Children play their part in the great College bazaar of 16 June, 1910, in order to raise money for the new hall, stage and screen.**

Above right: **As well as the practice Bishop Otter students also had to master the theory. This exam paper was tailored to the health and hygiene problems of the age.**

Below: **A class in 1914.**

FINAL EXAMINATION, 1913.

HYGIENE.

Tuesday, July 1st, 2.0–5.0.

Answer SEVEN *questions,* FIVE *questions from Section A. and* TWO *questions from Section B.*
N.B.—Technical terms should be avoided and answers should be illustrated by simple diagrams when practicable.

SECTION A.

1. What ill effects of defective vision, immediate and remote, may be observed or apprehended by the teacher in a child whose sight has been neglected? Mention any school circumstances which you think may tend to cause or increase defects of sight.

2. Describe briefly any deformities commonly met with among school children. State what can be done in school towards preventing or correcting such deformities.

3. Give a brief description in simple terms of the various purposes fulfilled by the blood.

4. Describe the methods you would adopt in teaching Hygiene in a practical way to children aged 7 to 8 years.

5. Mention some advantages which may be derived from the regular use of School Baths. Describe the type of bath you consider most satisfactory for this purpose, and give the reasons for your opinion.

6. What do you understand by the "centres" in the brain? What are their functions, and how are they linked up with the various parts of the body?

7. State briefly what you know of the chief means by which Tuberculosis is spread. In what ways is it possible through the School to diminish the liability of children to tuberculous infection?

8. A child 10 years of age has failed to make satisfactory progress since leaving the Infants' School. Mention any causes likely to account for this fact, and state what action you would take prior to an examination of the child by the Medical Inspector.

9. Mention any evils affecting the people as a whole which may result from the excessive drinking of alcohol.

SECTION B.

10. Describe the *Knee Raise* position and explain which are the essential and which the secondary points to be observed in teaching this position for the first time. What is the purpose of this exercise?

11. Mention the chief fault commonly met with in each of the following positions or movements and give your reasons for considering the fault to be of serious importance :—Head bending backward ; leg raising forward ; arms across bending ; hop march with leg raised backwards ; arms backward stretching ; prone falling.

12. Discuss briefly the various methods of making corrections when giving a lesson in Physical Exercises. State the occasions on which the different methods may suitably be adopted.

B 17388—50 Pk 907 4500 6/13

During the early 20th century Chichester's primary schools prospered and improved and Bishop Otter College students began to spend more of their teaching practice outside the College. The College School appears to have stopped being co-educational.

Above: **Dorothy Earl (student 1913-1915) taught this class of "Lanky Boys" (The Lancastrian School, Chichester), 1914.**

Below: **Dorothy Earl looking towards the camera, hop-picking with one of her *"Lanky Boys"*.**
Photographs kindly donated by Mr. I Robertson.

Left: **Kindergaten Certificate 1913.** *Maud Godwin's archives.*

In 1922 the Rev. Robert Fisher, Hon. Sec. to the College Council, declared

The great event... during the past year has been the closing of the Practising School and the acquisition of the buildings for the purposes of the College. This must, sooner or later, have happened, and the time was opportune. We are glad to be able to say that the teachers on the staff secured suitable appointments and nearly all the children found accommodation in the Central Church of England Girls' School.

Miss Chignell was thanked for her devoted service. Sad endings are often happy beginnings and the surplus accommodation was pressed into instant service as a recreation room, art block and other facilities.

Top photograph: **The new recreation room c. 1925.**

Centre and below: **Inside and outside the School block today (College Reception and Administration). The garden was reorganised by Dr. Brighton after the "Great Gale" of 1988.**

Chapter 6.
THE DEVELOPING CURRICULUM: FLORENCE JOHNSON'S COLLEGE 1919-1930

Students arriving at Bishop Otter College -1920

The train pulled into the station at Chichester and I struggled to pull trunks and boxes onto the platform. Several of us found ourselves in the same situation. A little man in a green apron appeared "Young ladies for Bishop Otter?", he enquired. "Yes" we murmured. Boxes, trunks and bags of all sizes went up onto the dray, and he handed us up to sit upon them. With a snap of his whip we were off, up South Street, round the Cross and into North Street. Curious glances were shot at us, but the driver seemed to find nothing strange in the method of our transportation. Into College Lane, and a glimpse of the grey buildings through the trees. My heart was beating fast and an air of apprehension gripped us all. We swung into the entrance of the College and the Principal was standing at the top of the steps. She wore a rather severe blue costume with white lace at her neck and in little ruffles around her wrists. Her hair was tied back into a bun and the sunlight gleamed thinly on her steel spectacles. My heart continued to thump and bump most uncomfortably. We were marshalled into a single line, and a voice hissed into my ear, "Walk up the steps, curtsey and say your name." The line moved forward, now was the moment. I walked up the steps and bobbed, "Miss Forster, Ma'am" I stuttered. "I welcome you into our family."

Above: **Personal recollections by former student E. Forster.**
BOC Archives.

54

It was not until the post-war era of the early '20s that something of Louisa Hubbard's vision for women began to be realised. Florence Johnson threw herself wholeheartedly into the new concepts of subject-specialism and departmentalism. Not only did the number of specialist staff increase during her ten years at the College, but the scope of the education was considerably widened. This was achieved both on and off campus and by the inauguration of educational links with Reading University and with other Training Colleges in Sussex and Hampshire.

A greater proportion of students went on to university after college to gain further qualifications and Miss Johnson's annual reports speak encouragingly of the ease with which her graduating students were finding work.

Below: **Miss Johnson in 1929.**

An urgent requirement, now that the College staff had
increased, was for improved living quarters. In 1923 a "Jubilee"
reunion of old students was held to celebrate the 50th anniversary
since the re-opening in 1873. *As a means of marking the event it was
proposed at the business meeting that a fund should be started for building
a necessary staff house. The proposal met with an immediate and
generous response, and it is hoped that before long the house will be
begun. It has long been realised that the present accommodation for the
lecturers and domestic staff is quiet inadequate and unworthy of the
College.* Florence Johnson, Report, 1924.

In 1926 the new staff accommodation (*below*) was opened,
leaving the old Principal's Residence (*above*) for the Principal, the
administration and the maids. The new staff house was furnished by
further fundraising from the Old Students' Guild.

Above: **Prefects, 1921.** Back row: left to right, standing: D. Jones, K. Jones, M. Petley, D. Darter, L. Wigg, L. Daly, L. Wallis. Front row: Left to right, seated, M. Locke, Principal Johnson, L. Watson.

Above: **Staff and senior students 1921.** Principal Johnson is seated centrally. On her right is Canon Fisher, secretary to the College Council, and on her left is Frederick Crowe, music master and organist at Chichester Cathedral.

This photograph is the last of the official year groups featuring senior students only (i.e. second years). After this the College began the still-current policy of taking a panoramic photograph each year of all students.

Attending to the inner person was part of Florence Johnson's new strategy for sound education.

Right: **Questions raised by the Board of Supervision as to the weekly cost of the College Board are hotly countered by Miss Johnson in her own defence, April 1925.**

Below: **The College dining hall circa 1910. It had probably not altered much by 1925.**

R Holland Esq.
National Society's Offices

April 27th 1925

Dear Mr. Holland

With reference to your enquiry re expences of Board, may I make the following explanation with regard to the cost in this College, viz., l0s 10 ¹/4d per head.

The dietary in this College is very plain, but varied, plentiful and well served. I feel very strongly that these things are essential to the well-being of the students, and I should be extremely reluctant to make any alteration. The dietary has been a matter of my close personal attention since I became Principal in 1919, and I am aware that the cost of board has increased; but the improvement has led to quite definite results:-

1. There has been practically no illness in the College during the last three years - no epidemic at all.

2. The standard of work has improved enormously, (I knew that H.M. Inspectors would bear me out in this) and this is I believe, in large measure caused by increased vitality due to better feeding.

3. The tone of the students has certainly been beneficially affected by the improvement in the dietary. Among other things I notice that there is practically no food brought into College by them.

I have a very efficient matron, and can guarantee that there is absolutely no waste here. I should at any time welcome an inspection of the domestic management. I will forward, if you wish, a copy of three weeks' dietary, as supplied to the Board of Education.

May I add that one of the reasons which has led me to increase the students' fees to the sum of £40 per annum has been my wish to maintain a high standard on the domestic side. I may say that Chichester is an expensive place to live in.

In the 1920s field trips became an essential part of the curriculum.

Left: Daphne Edwards is pictured about to set off on a biology field trip, complete with bike and collecting bucket.
Photograph reproduced from a sepia snapshop in Daphne Edwards's archive. In the background is the caretaker's cottage, (now in the black and white corridor).

Below: **For the first time in College life there were sufficient members of staff to make up a team. The first ever Staff v Students netball match took place on Monday 15 March 1926. The highlights of the days events were captured by student J McCanley who wrote in the College magazine:**

The Staff team turned out looking very neat and business-like (in spite of the fact that two of them were in borrowed plumes), and not a whit dismayed by the odds they were to face ... one or two had never played before whereas the students... had been 'brought up' on the game. An early failure to score was soon remedied after which one member of the Staff team now became a positive whirlwind. She... easily outdistanced everyone, including the ball and both umpires. Nothing daunted her, nothing could stay her career of victory. She ignored all minor details such as running with the ball, and refused to be restricted by the bounds of the court. Indeed, if the wire netting had not been there we should probably have lost her altogether.

The result was a creditable 13 to the Staff, 14 to the Students.

Photograph from Daphne Edwards's archives.

Art and craft in the twenties
Left: **In the art room 1926. College students pose with school children's work. Daphne Edwards's archives.**

Below: **Behind the art room doors a student's-eye view.**
College Magazine, 1926.

Before the pristine freshness of the first few days at College has had time to wear off, the Art Room has been robbed of its glamour. A smiling 'Second Year' takes the bewildered 'First Year' round the College, and her heart leaps at the words: "Now we'll go to the Art Room!" They enter a small room, which boasts two windows and a table, a gas ring and an ironing board, a sink and two kettles, and a zinc tub!
The plunge has been sudden, and the 'First Year' comes gasping to the surface, to hear her guide explaining, with pride in her voice: "We do everything here that we can't do anywhere else, you know. Ironing, hectographing, cooking, and a thousand and one odd jobs. This is the one room in the College where we can make a glorious mess with a clear conscience. I don't know what we should do without it! Drawing? Well, if you take my advice, you will not attempt to do any drawing here. This is the most popular room in College, and usually the most populous... There's the supper bell! We'll come in here afterwards and make some lemonade."

She chatters gaily on, but the light has died out of her companion's eyes; her most cherished dream is shattered.

Disillusionment is indeed a bitter draught!

P. Groom

Right: **The pottery kiln with Miss Wakefield (at rear) and students M. Plenty and V. King at front.**

Far right: **Students and Miss Wakefield examine their new pots with Principal Johnson, seated, looking on.**

The Arts and Crafts movement abroad in the country was enthusiastically followed in College both in works of art purchased for the chapel and elsewhere and in practical experimentation by the students. The kiln was located south of the former Practice School buildings in the courtyard.

Skill to do comes of doing, knowledge comes by eyes always open and working hands and there is no knowledge that is not power.
Motto on craft room wall, 1925

Above: **Left: Student Veronica Chambers prepares a model of a head (Miss Wakefield, psychology lecturer). Elaine Brogatski's archives, 1922-1924.**

Above: **Bookbinding in the craft room 1925-1927, from Daphne Edwards's archives.**

By 1928 students were also doing weaving, leather craft, lettering and illumination as well as woodcuts with which they illuminated the College Magazine.

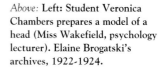

Left: **The two pottery photos were donated to the College among the archives of Violet Case.**

Drama

Drama maintained a high profile in College life in the twenties, as it had in the previous decade. In 1927 the College joined the Drama League and thereby gained greater access to modern plays for play readings.

However as the following extract from the College Magazine shows, drama was still certainly extra-curricular in 1928.

It was to our chagrin that we discovered that Juliet did Advanced Music on Wednesday while Romeo took Advanced Art on Friday and Mercutio was never available on Thursday afternoons!

Despite such rehearsal difficulties, however, the play was successfully staged for 3 performances at Christmas 1928.

Above: **Margaret Dawson and Noreen Hall pose for "the balcony scene".** The play was actually acted on stage in the hall where "many suggestions" were made to enable the immortal lovers to meet on the same plane, but tradition knows that they plighted their troth on a balcony, and so a balcony was constructed. This was painted by the Advanced Art Class and the love scenes (which had previously been rehearsed with Juliet perched perilously on a bracket) proceeded.

Left: ***Romeo and Juliet,*** **The Duel**

As well as the main public performances at Christmas and Easter the students also staged several plays and excerpts privately among themselves. In the academic year 1926-1927 *Much Ado about Nothing* and *Everyman* were presented to the public at Christmas and Easter. In November 26 the Guild Reunion was entertained with George Bernard Shaw's *Man of Destiny* by 2nd years while 1st years acted scenes from Antony and Cleopatra. In December the College chaplain helped with a short Christmas play, *The Miracle of Chimes*, while in the Easter Term the student Christian Union fund was augmented by money taken at the door for a performance of a short skit, *Mechanical Jane*. Three acts from George Bernard Shaw's *St. Joan* were also presented in the same term.

In June two performances were held in the garden. A touring company, Ben Greet's Company, performed scenes from *Twelfth Night* on 13 June. The College students themselves adapted and dramatised the medieval tale of *Aucassin and Nicolette*. The photograph (right) most probably shows rehearsals for *Aucassin and Nicolette* (Snapshot by Daphne Edwards who writes "This was abandoned as being too dangerous".)

Below: **Romeo and Juliet. The dying lovers and other members of the cast.**

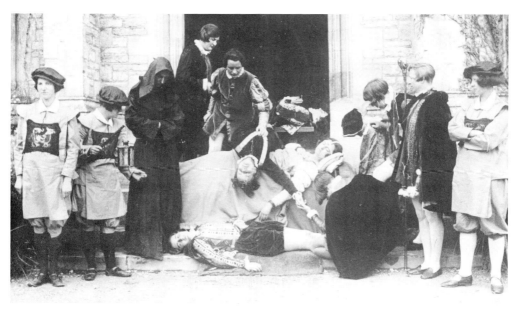

The Girl Guide movement was inaugurated in College following a visit in 1917 from Lady Baden Powell. By 1922 guiding was another of the extra-curricular College activities. It was an important landmark in women's emancipation. Cooking meals and fending for oneself in the open air was a long way from the suffocating drawing rooms from which Louisa Hubbard had striven to lead women away. The first 'Otter' camp appears to have been at Colworth near West Dean in 1922 and its participants wrote enthusiastically in the College Magazine on the joys of camp "to wake up at dawn and listen to the song of the birds so near" or at night, "the weird thrill of the night jar and the hoot of the owl". Many 'Otters' went on to become Rangers in order to take Guiding into the world beyond College as part of the broad teaching programme.
Photograph from Violet Case's archive.

Below: **Frederick Crowe and the Advanced Music Group, 1929.**

Frederick Crowe became organist and choir master at Chichester Cathedral in 1902. He founded the Cathedral Oratorio Society and helped inaugurate the Chichester Orchestral Society. He also had time for Bishop Otter College, attending to its music and choral teaching from 1906 onwards. Under his tutelage the College choir won eleven times out of thirteen competitions entered for the cup for best adult Choir in West Sussex. Mr Crowe retired in November 1930 and, sadly, died suddenly the following April. A plaque to his memory can be seen today in the cloisters.

In July 1930, shortly before Mr Crowe's death, Florence Johnson resigned her principalship to take up a new post as principal of St. Gabriel's College, London. The tributes from both staff and students were genuine and heartfelt while she herself expressed her "deep gratitude both for the happiness that we have shared together and for the promise which the future holds for our beloved College".

Chapter 7.
THE ACHIEVEMENTS OF THE '30s

FROM THE PRINCIPAL.

Miss Bazeley's Speech on Open Day.

June 17th, 1933.

MY LORD BISHOP, LADIES AND GENTLEMEN,

Those of you who have had the experience of building a new home for a large family on a very small income will understand a great deal of what we have been going through during the last two years.

If, when you have built your new house, you then proceed to move your family into it, and to live in both old and new houses at once, you will know that we did not undertake any easy exodus along a ready-made road into a promised land.

As a community we have had to make our road as we travelled; we have had to discover and adopt a new mode of life; we have had to develop all sorts of adaptability and resources which we scarcely knew we possessed in order to live up to the demands which our new way of life and our new opportunities have made upon us.

In the organisation of this great extension of the College buildings we have had many disillusionments and anxieties - we have taken upon us a burden of very heavy financial liability, which will be extremely difficult to meet. But there have been many compensations. We have all of us, (especially perhaps the Hon. Secretary, and the active Secretary and the Principal) learnt a great deal during the long process of building. We have learnt a great deal about work and workers, and I should like to say this that, amid all the crash of disillusionments, one figure has stood out with rock-like integrity, and that is the figure of the intelligent skilled workman. I want you to mark him well. I am not now thinking of the unskilled day-labourer – he is rather better than our social conditions and the less progressive of our schools make him. But I am thinking of the skilled, experienced, intelligent foreman – he has triumphed over all social conditions; he has used his education and gone far beyond it, yet remaining a homely, self-effacing person. He has great skill, he has wisdom and knowledge not only of his materials but of affairs and human beings. He has creative mind, and he works with individuality and with an artist's absorption in his work. He is modest, disinterested, honest; he does not let you down. I ask you to look at the staircases in the new Hall which were planned out and made by one of these workers. I invite you to go into the boiler house and contemplate the boilers – the work of another of our friends.

These skilled master workers know what is the end towards which they are working before they begin any particular job, and that, together with their unassuming reverence for their work, make perhaps two of the qualities which distinguish them from the day-labourer.

Why have I dwelt on these workers who have built the College? Because I very much hope that by some magic some of those qualities have been built into the spirit of this College – qualities such as their technical skill, their unassuming reverence for their work, their ability to see something of the end for which they are working.

You will not be surprised if I tell you that I like to think of a two year training college for young teachers such as ours, as a workshop rather than an academic institution. Our students are apprentices, we ourselves, the lecturers, are journeymen, our material – the medium in which we are learning to work - is life itself, and it is not only our material but also our master. We are concerned here and in all two year training colleges, not so much with books, with water-tight subjects and detached chunks of knowledge, as with learning how best to live helpfully in association with the children under our care in our schools.

E lsie Bazeley (left) succeeded Florence Johnson as Principal in September 1930 and immediately found herself engulfed in the preparations for extension of the College. The ground-work had been entirely Miss Johnson's who wrote in the College Magazine in July 1930.

The Extension Scheme has now reached a definite stage. Comprehensive plans have been drawn up which transform the New Wing [ie the 1901-1905 extension) into an educational block containing art and craft studies, a library and an extra science room. They involve the purchase of additional land, on which it is proposed to build a Hall of Residence with study bedrooms... and, if it can be carried out Bishop Otter College will rank amongst the most modern educational buildings in the country.

Elsie Bazeley took up the challenge and saw it through and, as her Open Day Speech (*opposite*) shows, turned it into an educational experience in itself.

New Hall was opened in September 1932 and contained study-bedrooms for 75 students, staff rooms, a common room, sick rooms and a principal's room. *A feature that excites much joy is that washing cubicles with running water (hot and cold) will be provided, one to every two students* remarked Elsie Bazeley in June 1931.

Left: The common room in New Hall, photographed in 1937.

Left: New Hall in 1980. The architects were messrs. Gutteridge and Gutteridge. A loan of £20,000 toward building costs was provided by the Central Board of Church Finance.

Unfortunately not all the students in College could get a new study-bedroom and two of the old cubicled dormitories remained in use for first-years.

With the opening of New Hall three former dormitories, Henty, Grosvenor and Ridgeway, were converted to an art room, geography room and library.

Below: **Former Ridgeway Dormitory opened in 1933 as the College library.** Despite this commitment to the expansion of the library, the College was still poorly equipped in this field. A meagre £30–£45 per annum was devoted in the annual budget to library stocks. There was no provision for staffing and it is not clear from the College records exactly how the resource was administered. It was not until 1939 that a member of staff, Miss F. H. Gwilliam, history lecturer, was designated as librarian. A further 7 years were to elapse before the college saw its first full time librarian. Miss M. J. Oughton commenced duties in January 1946 on a salary of £230 per annum. This was considerably less than a lecturer's salary but somewhat more than that of the average member of the administrative staff.

Below: **The old library prior to 1933.**

The College in 1932. Miss Bazeley is seated centrally, with dog in front. To her left in the picture is Miss Stella Westaway who stepped in as acting Principal for a term on Miss Bazeley's death in 1936.

Left: The College caretaker and his wife and dog. They also appear behind Miss Bazeley in the College photo above. They retired in 1933. The photo, donated by former student, Una Anderson, shows them outside the caretaker's house (now the women's cloakrooms in the black and white corridor). This continued as the caretaker's house until 1947 and was occupied by Harry Bell (*above*) their successor. Styled "College Bursar ", Mr Bell had the responsibility for a now greatly-extended college campus.

Below: **Play-group children on the terrace with ex-principal Miss Johnson (centre) and Principal Bazeley (back to camera).**

Bottom: **Students' account of the new play centre. Magazine, 1932.**

The great theme of all our college work now is the study of the child, the child not only in school, but the child as a human being, the child as a member of society, the child as a developing personality, changing all the time from the cradle and nursery school up to and beyond senior school days. The students study the children at play, indoors and out of doors, on the sand pile, and in the little Red Indian gang, and not only under instruction in the classroom. They try to acquaint themselves with the natural interests of children so that the education in school can move along natural lines and not along rigid and artificial lines. The students are beginning to acquire an insight into children's minds and hearts and needs, and they are beginning to acquire the elements of skill and of technique as teachers; they are adding to their own knowledge and carrying it forward in the advanced courses in some special direction, whether of history, science, art music or what not.

(Elsie Bazeley 1933)

Miss Bazeley's chief legacy to the College was that she reintroduced young children inside its gates. A play-centre was set up with the dual aim of developing children's free expression and helping the students understand the child. The centre was funded by a-penny-a-week donations from old students which were collected and administered by Mavis Alchorn

(For her photo see Cricket XI on p. 72)

THE PLAY CENTRE.

The idea of starting a Play Centre at College arose from some visits paid to London Play Centres in January 1931, and the Students opened our Play Centre during the following term.

Our first children were those living in the tin huts at the bottom of the College Lane. We chose these children, our nearest neighbours, thinking that the space we could provide would be specially welcome to children whose surroundings at home were so confined. These children are still with us and we have now added several families recommended by St. Pancras School.

At present we have just over fifty regular attendants, somewhat reinforced on fine Summer evenings when the additional space in the hockey field enables us to relax some of our stern regulations against "gate crashers." If we had yielded to our natural impulses all the children of Chichester would by now have "Joined the Children's College."

The first evening still lingers in our memories. The Craft Room was transferred into a Nursery with low tables, flowers and toys; the Blue Common Room was a play-room for older children, and the Geography Room became a library with arm-chairs round the fire. Even the potting shed was drawn into service and contained bowls of hot water, towels and scented soap! The popularity of other occupations waxes and wanes, but hot water has never lost its charms.

At first the children stood and gazed about them; then almost simultaneously the babies seized wheeled toys and ran round and round with them as if trying to realise the space. After about ten minutes they chose toys and settled down quietly. The older children took rather longer to lose their shyness, but by the third evening were completely at home. At all times these older ones have shown great consideration for our property, both indoors and out, and are always volunteering to help us with the putting away of toys and the care of the younger children.

We have not made much effort to organise the children's play, preferring that they should select their own activities and that organisation should arise from real needs. Toys are always popular with the younger children, and for a long time many of the older girls preferred dolls to any other play. We are always in need of toys and are most grateful for any cast off ones which the pupils of our old students have sometimes sent us. Dolls and tea-sets, trains, wheeled toys, bats, balls and skipping ropes are among the favourites. Library books are also in great demand.

After a long illness our late Principal, Miss E T Bazeley, has passed to her rest. She was an inspiring and undaunted teacher; devoted to her work; and all on fire. No student who has spent her full course with Miss Bazeley as Principal, is likely to forget her enthusiasm and the sheer love of her craft… Her influence will long be felt wherever her students are to be found.
George, Bishop of Chichester, Chairman of College Council, December 1936.

Miss Bazeley died in 1936 but the work she had started with young children in College was taken up with considerable enthusiasm by the incoming Principal, Dr Dorothy Meads. She asked for more funds for the scheme, explaining that twice a week for an hour more than a hundred children of all ages came to the College and were able to develop and express themselves. Her only regret was that, due to lack of time, they could not provide similar centres for boys and girls who had left school.

The photos on this page have been reproduced from the College Magazines of 1933 and 1935 and show the "College baby" (*above*); play centre children (taken by 1935-1937 students J Ray and J Brandon) left; the boys club and college bursar, Harry Bell (*below*).

Above: **The Cricket XI, Summer 1932. Left to right: Joan Bootherstone, Doris Fairbairn, Peggy Braddock, Betty Coombes, Toby Fiander, Kathleen Kent (standing). Eunice Main, Mabell Purscell, Sylvia Latham (captain), Mavis Alchorn, Joyce Coombes (seated).**

Below: **Tennis, netball, rounders and hockey teams 1938-1939.**

Left: **Open Day, 7 June 1932.** Country dancing on the lawn.

Incoming Principal, Dr. Dorothy Meads, was anxious to expand the educational facilities of the College by providing certain advanced courses. In 1936-7 eleven acres immediately south of the College gardens came on the market "including the field so long used for hockey". They were purchased and thus the College's potential for sports and physical education was much enhanced. Next, in order to meet the Board of Education criteria for the advanced course in physical training, it was decided to build a proper gymnasium. Architect Stanley H. J. Roth of 6, East Pallant was engaged and the building was completed in 1939. The new course was approved by the Board and by Reading University.

Plans for further College expansion were immediately set in hand and in May 1939 a new post of consulting architect to the College was created. Unfortunately, however, the interruption of World War II meant that Dr. Meads's plans were to remain unrealised in her own life time.

The academic staff of the College now numbered 15 together with the chaplain, the Rev. Canon A.R. Browne Wilkinson, and an administrative staff of 5 including the librarian.

Above: **The new gymnasium inside and out. The second floor provided additional study bedrooms. The cost of building the gym meant that a scheme for a Bazeley Memorial Paddling Pool for playcentre children was, sadly, shelved indefinitely.**

Left: Aerial view showing the entire College campus at the close of the 1930s: new staff house (1925) on extreme left; the core of 19th century buildings with 1901 additions centre; gymnasium (1938) east of the chapel; New Hall (1933) top right.

Below: **Dr. Meads** seated, a little left of centre, with the College at the close of the decade, July 1939.

Chapter 8.
WORLD WAR II
AND THE
RETURN TO EDEN
1941-1947

A.419590/42/W.6.a.2.   A.M. Form 1553.

An Agreement made the seventeenth day of August
1943 BETWEEN Bishop of Chichester & the Archdeacons of
Chichester and Lewes,
of   West Dean, Vicarage, Chichester, Sussex.
of the one part and THE SECRETARY OF STATE FOR AIR
(hereinafter called " the Department ") of the other part.

Insert   WHEREAS the Department has taken possession of all
description
of the   those premises known as Bishop Otter Memorial College,
property.   College Lane, Chichester, Sussex,

pursuant to the powers conferred on it by the Defence Regulations
1939 by reason of which compensation is or will be payable to the
said the Bishop of Chichester and the Archdeacons of Chichester
and Lewes
under the provisions of the Compensation (Defence) Act 1939.

It is hereby agreed between the parties hereto that the Department
shall pay and the said Bishop of Chichester and the Archdeacons
of Chichester and Lewes
shall accept payment at the rate of £ 2,700 (two thousand, seven hundred
pounds)
per annum payable quarterly on the usual quarter days in satisfaction of the sums which may be payable pursuant to Section
2 (1) (a) and of interest thereon under Section 10 of the said Act.
The said compensation shall be payable as from and including
the   **thirtieth** day of   August,   19 42

AS WITNESS the hands of the parties hereto.

Witness to the signature of the   George Worth:
Beatrice May Bishop   Bishop of Chichester   C.P.S. Clark (Archdeacon of
S. Hill's Drive,   Chichester)
Chichester: Spec.Asst   Hamilton Smythe (Archdeacon of
                                                                   Lewes)

Witness to the signature of
P. E. ROWLINSON
on behalf of the SECRETARY OF STATE
FOR AIR
J.A. Hill, Air Ministry, London.   M.S. Hamilton.

R.A.F. OCCUPATION OF THE COLLEGE

Bishop Otter College was occupied by the Royal Air Force from August, 1942, to May, 1945. It was first used to house some five hundred members of the Women's Auxiliary Air Force who were employed in the Royal Air Force Tangmere Sector Operations Room, then established in St. James' Road Infant School, Chichester. When the rapid expansion of air operations made it necessary to find a larger room, the College hall was adapted for the purpose, and the Tangmere Sector Operations Room was transferred thither on 15th February, 1944, and fully staffed from that date until the end of 1944. The hall was extensively used during the preparatory phase before the invasion of Normandy to control aircraft on escort duties, intruder operations, attacks on transport and lines of communication, aerodromes and flying bomb sites and other tactical targets. During the invasion of Normandy, which began on 6th June 1944, fifty six squadrons taking part in the invasion were controlled from this room. From January to May, 1945, the hall was maintained as an Emergency Operations Room, with a reduced staff, directing and controlling fighter aircraft in action against flying bombs.

A commemorative plaque, worded as above, was installed in the Hall shortly after the War had
ended. Unfortunately it has since been removed or boarded up and is no longer traceable.

In purchasing the extra land to the south of the College (below) Dr. Meads had hoped for a rapid expansion in the College's educational capacity. All such plans were, however, forestalled by World War II. RAF Tangmere began to look for a suitable building with a large hall in the vicinity of their aerodrome and eventually Bishop Otter College was chosen.

In the summer of 1942, immediately after final exams, the staff and students were evacuated and 500 WAAFS were installed in

their place. With no time to find suitable premises for the evacuees, BOC was forced to go to Stockwell College in Bromley, very near London, and itself recently evacuated! BOC was "indignant, but helpless to take any action". What no-one in the College knew then, for it was top secret, was that the College hall was to be used to mastermind the D-Day operation. Retrospectively, though worn out with the worry of caring for her flock amid the London bombs, Dr Meads was proud to have helped the war effort in this way.

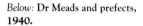

Below: **Dr Meads and prefects, 1940.**

During the first two years of World War II the students and staff prepared to dig in at the College. By October 1939, three air raid shelters had been constructed in the grounds, each capable of sheltering 56 persons. In November 1939 it was agreed to dig up part of the grounds in order to grow potatoes. By 1942 it was reported to the Finance Committee that the students were producing "more than sufficient vegetables to supply almost the total College needs", and two women workers were taken on to tend the vegetable plots on a full time basis. Classrooms were filled to capacity as students from Portsmouth Training College, devastated by air raids, joined in with BOC students. Bishop Otter College also responded to the Country's call by volunteering for the Red Cross, and drills and parades were conducted in the grounds. In the air raid shelters students were taught how to put out incendiary bombs.

Above: **Physical exercise 1941. Photographs donated by 1940-1942 student Freda Martens (née Barr) who says they were dressed in beige blouses and dark brown pleated shorts. The rectangular building on the left of the photograph is the air-raid shelter.**

*Below:*Red Cross Inspection, 1941.
College postcard series.

Since 1901 when the hall was first built it had been widened to the north, to provide a large square area that the RAF found suitable to their needs. Two large 'plotting tables' were placed centrally with desks all around and a purpose built observation gallery aloft.

Three 'in-house' RAF magazines have survived in the College archives. In one of them the new residents regret that they have had to dislodge the students and "... it is to be hoped that it will not be long before the buildings are returned to their life's work, which has of necessity been so cruelly interrupted." (August 1944). The renowned sense of humour which helped carry so many RAF pilots to victory, and often to their death, shines through in the excerpt below from one of the RAF magazines, in which Otter's gambling den, complete with croupiers, is immortalised.

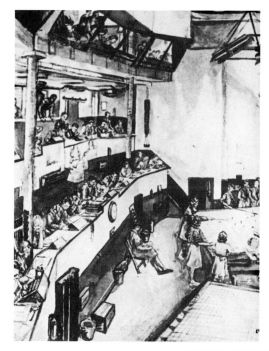

The Bishop founded his seminary towards the end of the nineteenth century chiefly for the purpose of instructing young women in the arts of conducting gambling hells. Some of the original croupiers' rakes have been unearthed, together with a number of coloured counters. This seems odd conduct for a bishop. But a fragmentary manuscript discovered in the ruins of the College reveals the bishop as altogether an odd bird. The manuscript has been deciphered as follows :—

He crept from his crypt, did the good Bishop Otter,
　　Inspired with an urge for new knowledge.
He stole to the Rest Room and said to a plotter,
　　" Pray, what's going on in my College ? "

In thinking the Waaf would be scared, he's mistaken ;
　　She winked and said " Ssh—careless chatter ! "
The Bish was the one who was pretty much shaken
　　As she took him aside for a natter ;

And dating him up at the Dolphin, the plotter
　　Said, beckoning one of the waiters,
" The thing that thrills me about you, Alfy Otter
　　'S the wizard design of your gaiters."

The evening progressing, the Bish grew elated
　　And even the Waaf showed surprise
When he said " Tho', of course, you are quite pixillated,
　　I think you've got lovely brown eyes."

It is perhaps as well that no more of this manuscript remains.

Above and right **Artistic impressions of the hall with D-Day preparations in progress by WAAF telephonist, E. Baker, 1944.**
Above right: **The Hall in the early 1950s with war-time observation gallery still in place.**
(*College Postcard series*)

14

Flt/Lt. Cooke has again offered a book token prize for the best verse of not more than fourteen lines on some aspect of Operations. Entries should be placed in the box in the Guardroom, B.O.C., not later than September 15th.

Here is Cpl. Finch's prize-winning entry :—

BOMBER TRACKS

On the long night watch I sit and think of you,
And when I see the bombers coming back
I pray that one of them is yours and bless
The arrows of each safely homing track.

(I hear you drumming through the night-dark sky
Another danger past, a journey done,
Another day ahead to live and laugh,
To eat, and sleep, and linger in the sun).

The tracks move up the table, cross the coast,
The Filter Room, the plotters do their part—
But no one sees those wings beside your wings—
What symbol could they use to plot my heart ?

HELEN FINCH.

—:o:—

In October 1944 the RAF magazine editor reported a heavy loss on previous production costs and regretted that, as these had been met out of the Canteen Fund, this was a subsidy that could not continue. The magazine was now to cost 9d. a month.

We are deeply indebted to editor L.A.C. Green's struggle to publish; for without his efforts the three years of RAF occupation of the College would be a colourless statement of fact. Instead the magazine provides us with flesh and bones; wartime personnel continuing on the same enthusiastic lines as the students before them - dances in the Assembly Rooms at Chichester; shows in aid of the Red Cross and the St. John Fund. The WAAFs, the Operations Personnel, the Signals Corps and ATS differed only from the usual residents of the College in that some of them were bound to die in the course of their work.

Above: **poem from RAF Magazine, September 1944.**

Left: **WAAF Doreen Preston and friends.**

" 'D DAY ' AT BISHOP OTTER COLLEGE "

Here in this place, where " D Day " moves are planned,
Calmness prevails ; no noisy demonstration,
No outward show, to give an intimation,
Of what we know and feel, this Sixth of June.

The Operations Room is quietly manned
By democratic peoples ; sisters, brothers,
Calmly composed, controlling lives of others ;
And, ... which the Hun would fail to understand,
The tennis-court's still booked this afternoon.
The Tables show the sky is thickly dotted
With aerial might of every Allied Nation,
God's answer to His people's supplication
Is seen in each swift silent movement plotted.

ANON.

—:o:—

Mr. Wootton is all in faviour
Of General Montgomery's behaviour.
He's longing for the day, of course,
When there'll be no more civilians in the Royal Air Fourse.

Above right: **WAAF Doreen Preston continues to dig for victory as the College students had done before her in the early years of the war. New Hall, in which the WAAFs were billeted, is in the background. 500 WAAFs were squeezed in by use of bunks rather than proper beds.**

Above Left: **Poem from RAF magazine (edited by L.A.C. G.W. Green and published by kind permission of Wing Commander D. Hamilton Grice, DFC).**

Left: **WAAF Doreen Preston and friend prove the point of the poem above: it may be war, but the tennis courts are still booked!**

As well as tennis, table tennis and badminton played on site for relaxation, there were RAF/BOC football and cricket teams playing home and away. Not only Tangmere and other RAF sites, but the community at large was visited. On 17 September 1944, for instance, Stanstead Park CC was beaten by RAF/BOC by 51 runs at Lord Bessborough's ground.

BISHOP OTTER COLLEGE, CHICHESTER
TELEPHONE: 2150

PRINCIPAL: MRS D M MEADS, MA PHD (LONDON)
26th June, 1944
Dear Mr. Fisher,

We had a very bad night - the pilotless 'planes i. e. f lying bombs coming over with very little pause all through the hours of darkness (this is now the twelfth day and night), and we had some close shaves. At 4. 30am we became a Rest Centre, and had to feed 170 odd at breakfast, and they are still coming. If I told you what had happened, I should be giving away secrets.

We had a few hours' lull this morning, but, since 12.30, they have been passing over the College incessantly, with only two or three minutes between, falling very close. The blast is fatal.

I am sending First Year students home: the noise and chaos in the College are indescribable. The telephone, children crying, spotter's whistles and bells, and our own lack of sleep make one feel as though one is in a madhouse - not to mention the P planes overhead.

But First Years have had to go, because the homeless have taken possession of the West shelter, and tonight Second Years must sleep in the one small shelter allocated to us. We are now having to do exams in a flimsy hut - as the classrooms on the ground floor, protected by blast walls, are all occupied by the homeless. We are in the middle of Finals, with this afternoon's paper interrupted every five minutes!

I rang up the Board of Education. They did not sound particularly sympathetic, and remarked that I must arrange for the students' work elsewhere if I sent them home, otherwise we should be in 'grant' difficulties. In face of this great menace, it does not seem to matter very much. My Fleet Air Arm brother had heard rumours, and got leave from Midhurst to come and see me. He was only in the place an hour - but he was horrified at what was happening. But how can I abandon Finals?

I do not know if it will be possible for me to leave the College and attend the Finance Committee next week. In haste,

Kindest regards, Yours sincerely

Dorothy M Meads Principal.

Rev R Fisher

28th May, 1944.

My Lord and Members of the Council,

The last meeting of the Council on March 10th, empowered me to take whatever action I thought best in any emergency created by Air Raids. Throughout most of last term we had an exhausting time, due to the frequency of successive night alerts, accompanied by heavy and prolonged gun-fire and, on occasions, by bombs. The Spring term is never an easy one because Final School Practice, and the Final Inspection of Practical Teaching takes place in it, and that, in itself, creates a feeling of strain. Now there is added, for students, the unremitting Fire Watching and Fire Drill, rehearsals for Rest Centre, and much domestic work - washing up, laying tables, preparing vegetables, cleaning their own rooms. Last term the climax came on the night of March 15th, when, in addition to the usual showers of incendiaries, four bombs fell very close indeed to the College, causing fatal casualties in the neighbourhood and a very considerable amount of destruction. (This was after several weeks of broken nights and evenings.) On the following day, we decided, at a Staff meeting, to disperse the students to their several homes, two weeks earlier than we had originally intended, and to set them to do, at home, a very full programme of reading and essay work, to be submitted to the Staff by a definite date. Hence, the students dispersed on March 18th instead of April 1st.

Further heavy and unpleasant raids during the next two weeks justified, I think, the steps we had taken.

With the usual few exceptions the students did their work at home well, and they certainly returned on April 22nd very much refreshed, and settled down most purposefully. And except for four brief Alerts in the first week of the term, and reverberations from the Channel, no Siren or any untoward incident has so far disturbed the peace. The unbroken evenings and nights have been most beneficial to study, and to the general atmosphere, for the students feel now that there is every probability, when they settle down in the evening to a piece of work, that they will be able to complete it undisturbed. One can realise now what havoc the constant Sirens of the past year have played in the academic preparation of students for their profession.

"Letters from Principal Dorothy Meads, in Bromley, to the College Council in Chichester."

The miseries of war so graphically described by Dorothy Meads in confidential letters to her Council (opposite page) were to some extent offset by the elegance of the College's new surroundings at Bromley. The lake was especially appreciated.

Top Left: **The Old Palace, Bromley, home to Bishop Otter College September 1942 - June 1945. Its usual occupants, Stockwell College, had themselves been evacuated to the country.**

Left: **Dorothy Meads with "Mary" and "Solomon" photographed by Miss M. Eele, lecturer in music. Reproduced from a photograph in the College Magazine, 1948.**

Below: **Excerpt from Dr. Meads's letter to students past and present, May 1945.**

Today the atmosphere is one of quiet thankfulness for the miracle of Victory in Europe.

Linked with our thanksgiving for this stupendous achievement is also deep gratitude that the College buildings at Chichester have survived intact to await our return although, for many months before and D-Day itself, this was the secret centre from which all the most vital invasion operations were planned... Victory in Europe in due time bring to a triumphant conclusion our stay in the Old Palace. To its little Chapel, its classrooms and study bedrooms, its vibrating 18th Century Centre, its strong shelters and blast walls, its lake and gardens, we are truly grateful.

Harry Bell, the College Steward, had stayed on site during the war as "clerk of works" liaising between the College and the RAF. There was considerable cleaning to do before the College could return (including cockroaches to be exterminated from the kitchens). Audrey Bell, later his wife (née Read), came to College as Assistant Domestic Bursar in 1945 and recalls postwar rationing in which each student collected a ration of fat and sugar and a pot of jam or marmalade each month,—*they collected them at the kitchen door but often dumped them round the College and forgot them.*

Top and centre left: **Gymnastics and Chorals in the grounds,? 1946-7.**
Bottom left: **Open Day 1947. Display of national dancing. Dance and free movement was now part of the official curriculum.**

BISHOP OTTER COLLEGE
DUTIES OF LECTURER IN CHARGE

The week's duties of the Lecturer-in-Charge of the College run from Monday morning to Saturday dinner-time.

The actual duties of the Lecturer-in-Charge include, amongst others:

1. *The supervision of the work of the College Orderlies, and discussion with them of any untidiness or neglect of the library, classrooms, corridors, etc.*

2. *The care of the College and Staff Registers, and the Staff Meetings Minute Book.*

3. *The clearing, and keeping tidy and up-to-date, of the notice boards in the covered cloister and corridor, other than the Union Notice Board. The 'Today' board should have daily attention.*

4. *Arranging for, and supervising the preparation of Large Hall, Common Room, and Classrooms, when needed for functions, examinations, outside lectures, exhibitions, etc.*

5. *To take Chapel one evening in the week, and at such other times as requested.*

6. *To see the Principal each morning and to keep her in touch with the general day-to-day organisation of the College.*

7. *To receive visitors to the College, unless these wish to see the Principal personally.*

8. *To assist in keeping down the electric light bill, by drawing the attention of the College Orderlies to carelessness in this direction.*

9. *To make sure that Miss Best is aware of any change in routine affecting domestic arrangements, such as visitors staying for a meal, or for the night.*

The Deputy Principal takes the place of the Principal in the latter's absence and at other times as arranged and needed.

Dorothy M Meads Principal

30th October 1945

BOC Archives MS 14/3

Above: **The children re-establish themselves in College. The "eleven strange huts" the Nissen huts, left over from the war, were converted into art and craft rooms.**

The return to Chichester was fraught with difficulties. Rooms were not ready. Some RAF personnel were still on site. Due to the shortage of trained teachers the Ministry persuaded BOC to raise the students numbers to 200, but there was nowhere to accommodate the extra numbers. For the first time lodgings in Chichester were hired including accommodation for 14 in the Bishop's Palace itself, due to the kindness of Bishop and Mrs Bell. Out of 14 full-time lecturers only 3 had been with the College before the move to Bromley. Dramatic productions were hampered by the lack of stage, screen, curtains or adequate lighting - all had been ripped out in the war effort. Nevertheless, the College gradually rehabilitated itself and the compensation money from the Ministry of Defence helped pay for some of the refurbishment.

Excerpt from the Bishops' Address on the return of B.O.C. to its "home", 1945.

... Linked with the Cathedral and the Palace, and in an environment with special charms of its own, Bishop Otter College weaves a spell which no student can ever forget....On behalf of the Council I should like to thank the Principal and Staff for their resolute spirit and indefatigable labours during the safari to Bromley....Above all, I wish the College a prosperous and happy year, in the familiar surroundings in 1946.
BOC. Archives A57/90

The strains of the war years and the difficulties of the return to college took their toll on Dr. Meads's health. In 1945 a heart condition was giving her cause for concern and in due course, at Christmas 1947 she retired due to ill-health. The tributes in her praise, regret at her departure mixed with sympathy for her condition, were warm and sincere. They stressed her courage, her determination, her administrative ability and, above all, her humanity, her willingness to listen and to offer help, to staff and students alike. Dr. Meads died in 1958.

Below: **Dr. Meads and her war time flock. An undated year group,? 1942.**

Chapter 9.
THE BROADENING HORIZON: DR. MURRAY'S COLLEGE 1948-1970

When she came to Bishop Otter in 1948 she found a Church Training College (to use the old title, which sounds dated now), flourishing but small in size and restricted in its scope and intention. No doubt in taking on an assignment which lay outside her previous experience, she could not envisage what was in store for her. Perhaps it was just as well, or she might have had second thoughts. Fortunately for us, she came, and over the years revealed a capacity which matched all the increasing demands which the College was to make in an ever-changing situation.

Roger Chichester.

Part of the Bishop's tribute to Betty Murray in 1970, on her retirement.
(College Report 1969-70).

Authors' Apology
We live today in a world of visual record. This wealth has also its negative side. It has rarely seemed worthwhile for photographers of College life in recent years to collect the names of their subjects, as was so often done in the past. The College archives from the '50s to the '80s are the poorer for it. It seems unsatisfactory not to be able to put names to faces in the following, and some of the previous pages. The photos are therefore used with thanks, and apologies, to those who may recognize themselves in them.

The College in 1948.

K. M. E. (Betty) Murray, Fellow and Junior Bursar of Girton College, Cambridge, came to Bishop Otter College as Principal in 1948. She was immediately faced with the challenge of Dr. Meads's unfulfilled dream, that of modernizing and expanding the College. In practical terms this meant that students had to have proper study facilities. New hostels were therefore immediately planned. Provision for a new Chapel, dining hall, kitchens, a second gym, students' common room and a music room followed close on their heels. All these were planned, financed, built and in use during Miss Murrays' principalship. By 1960 the College was co-educational and was about to embark on the new 3-year training course. In 1964 the Robbins Report was welcomed for its proposal to provide a 4-year BEd. course and, regretfully, the 40-year link with Reading University was severed in order to forge new links with the University of Sussex. Academic Board, Faculty Board and Departmental Meetings were established in order to give the ever-expanding staff a chance to be properly involved in academic policy.

Above left: **Miss Murray pictured in 1948 with old Students.** *Anon.*

Above right: **Bishop Bell at Open Day, c. 1956.**

Miss Murray retired in 1970 and pursued an active life in the community, giving her talents to the Society of Sussex Downsmen and the Sussex Archaeological Society among other causes, while publishing, in 1977, a biography of her grand-father, first editor of the Oxford English Dictionary. She received her honorary doctorate from Sussex University in 1978 for her services to education.

One of Miss Murray's close friends and allies in her early years at the College was Bishop George Bell, Bishop of Chichester 1929-1958. At his death in 1958 she expressed the sorrow felt by the College by saying, *In a wonderful way he always seemed to have time to do for us whatever we wanted of him - preaching a sermon, giving a lecture, coming to Open Day, patiently seeking a solution to some special problem.*

Bishop George Bell believed that the greatest thing to be learned at College was the art of living in a social group. *The common life calls for the exercise of social qualities: give and take, consideration of the common interest, absorbing the common tradition. There is a history in the college which you inherit, a tradition which you not only receive but enrich.*

(Sermon delivered at the Annual Service in Chichester Cathedral, 5 October 1948.)

He indeed practised what he preached and threw himself into the communal life of the College.

In many ways the clubs and societies at BOC were little changed from those of the pre-war years. The Rambling Club, French Circle, Dramatic and Literary Society, Guide Club, Film Society and others all used for space in the magazine pages. There was even a Rabbit Club (breeding rabbits for their fur!)

Above: **Bishop Bell entertains, c. 1953. The staff sitting in the front row are as follows left to right:**

Miss McCririck (Art); Miss M. Miller (Education: pearl necklace); Dr. Murray; Miss Howell (Vice Principal: starred dress); Miss Morgan (Left of Bishop); Miss Sterry (Biology: in white); Agnes Sibley (USA Exchange: hand to mouth); and Bishop Bell, standing.

Below: College dance c. 1953. The College students were allowed to invite the man of their choice to such occasions.

The strong College tradition of working and learning with children was pursued through the '50s. College staff included a full-time lecturer in Infant and Nursery Education.

The photographs here, all circa 1953, show a range of activities from the day out, (top left: the bus waits at the College gates) to a Christmas party at Oaklands House.(*left*).
The two photographs above show agility training for youngsters on the College campus - encouraged as part of a programme for healthy all round development of children.

Standards of excellence were achieved in needlework in the early '50s under the tutelage of Mrs. E. Massey (later Mrs. Thomas), lecturer in Needlework 1948-1953.

1950

1951

The top right photograph shows students at work. The remaining photographs show students in Summer '49, '50, and '51 modelling their " final assessment" pieces. The dresses each had to be designed and made by the students who also submitted a theory paper on some related topic.

Photos donated by Mrs. Thomas, who now lives at Fishbourne.

1949

93

THE ART COLLECTION

The College's fine collection of modern, largely British Art, began to be collected after the Second World War. The seeds were sown by the Principal, Dorothy Meads, who encouraged her Head of Art, Eleanor Hipwell, to consider the loan and purchase of pictures to be hung in College. In 1947 three original works were purchased from an exhibition in the Victoria and Albert Museum - a gouache, *Desert Flowers*, by Kathleen Moss, a lithograph, *Hares*, by Margaret Horder and a watercolour, *Figure holding Autumn leaves*, by Michael Rothenstein. Only the last artist has acquired something of a reputation today.

The real growth of the collection began with the arrival of Betty Murray as Principal in 1948 . Her drive, coupled with that of her newly appointed lecturer in art, Sheila McCririck, saw the continuous purchase of works by distinguished artists of the day. Encouraged by Bishop George Bell, Chairman of the College Council and, after 1955, by the new Dean of Chichester, himself a patron of artists, Walter Hussey, the College approached up-and-coming artists.

In 1959 Betty Murray wrote to Henry Moore and Ivon Hitchens. Moore had nothing suitable to offer the College at that point; Hitchens, whose studio was in West Sussex, responded as follows.

The position appears to be that you might pay a hiring fee of £10 a year, as do the Arts Council and British Council but this would not get you very far, and as you have a constantly changing audience a permanent collection supplemented occasionally - would give you least trouble.

On the other hand you don't want artists' second best pictures - nor is it fair to ask painters to lend their best and saleable work for long periods of one or 2 years, as the modern painter is mostly hard pressed financially, and another difficulty in lending is the absence of much needed frames.

Why don't you buy two pictures a year on the instalment plan at £25 a year each. Thus in 2 years the painters would be £50 in pocket and you would have four permanent pictures in 4 years, - or the painters might be content with £10 a year. In which case you could start off with five pictures and the collection would soon build up.

If you only hire you will have constant expense in transport and insurance and little to show for it - while there is still a chance, that with a permanent collection you may be able to borrow occasional shows from the Arts Council. If you know the artists you want - then you can write them personally direct - by selling direct to you, they will be saving the dealers' commission 33¹/₃%. Thus for instance I could personally let you have a 75 guinea picture for 50 guineas - or call it £50. In writing to me I take it that you have had this in mind and I should be very glad to help you by spreading the payment over several years but preferably not more than two.

If you see the London exhibitions ? you may know whose pictures you want - or if I see something that strikes me as cheap and particularly worthwhile on my occasional visits round shows - I could let you know.

Would you care to come and talk it over when we get home about August 21st.

There is a good bus service if you haven't a car. £50 is quite a valuable asset and carefully selected you could pick up a valuable collection like that.

So the College acquired *Autumn Stream* by Hitchens and his invaluable advice became a guide for the future policy in building the collection.

In 1950 Betty Murray wrote to Bishop Bell:

I am writing, as you said I might, to remind you that we should be very grateful if you could give us an introduction to Graham Sutherland. We set aside £50 a year to buy original pictures and have purchased three through the C.E.M.A. exhibition of pictures for schools, and now this one of Ivon Hitchens. We feel that it is very important that students who are going to teach in all grades of primary and secondary modern schools, and who come, for the most part, from rather ordinary homes without much cultural background, should be helped from the surroundings we give them in College to form standards of their own. We take them to exhibitions in London and elsewhere, as far as possible, but this is not the same thing as living with good examples of contemporary art, and, given material, I think the College has a contribution to make here in the education of public taste. The students themselves have asked that, if possible, the next picture we buy should be one by Graham Sutherland. . .

Following this contact, 5 students and 5 staff were invited to view paintings in Sutherland's studio. The students recorded the occasion:

...Eventually after a difficult process of elimination (we) came away with Entrance to a Lane, chosen because it is so peaceful and we hope it will prove timeless.

The first sculpture to enter the Collection was Willie Soukop's *Mother and Child* in polyphant stone. Soukop followed his work to the College when he came as visiting lecturer in "*Contemporary Sculpture*" in 1952-53.

Other paintings and sculptures followed fast including a small seated figure in bronze by Henry Moore and paintings and drawings by Feibusch, Moore, Scott, Spencer, Paul Nash, Bowden, Rouault, Lanyon, Gear, Wallis, Stern, Bratby, etc.

Above: **Mother and Child by** Willie Soukop.

Below: **Bronze. *Seated figure on steps*. Maquette by Henry Moore.**

Black and White by Patrick Heron.

One of a set of 4 jugs by Alison Britton.

Photographed by Dave Turner.

96

Art in College was not only for viewing, but, more especially, for doing. By 1961 the lecturer in art, Sheila McCririck had been joined by a second full-time lecturer in art, Miss Mather. Among other creative skills, weaving, woodwork and pottery still had their own full-time lecturers, while dyeing and fabric printing were additional skills acquired in the Art Room.

Top right: '50s students brighten up the Nissen Huts with murals. Hut 6 was first attempted - depicting the journey of the river from hills to the sea and of the road from country to town. Next, in Hut 8, London and Paris were painted.

Centre right: Spinning and weaving in the Nissen Huts. Miss D. Middleton was lecturer in weaving for many years during the period.

Below: By the '60s the practice of art had found space and light in new premises in the 1901 wing (now the Mitre Art Gallery).

The '50s also saw the arrival of students from overseas. As well as the chaplain, Canon Eperson (seated just left of centre), two male members of staff have been appointed, James Donaghy (education and psychology) and D.W. Shave (geography). The new male students are on the right of the group (bottom photograph).

Below: **1957. Male students make their first appearance in the College ranks.**

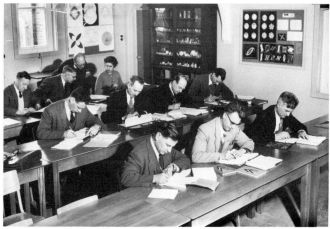

By 1960 there were 50 men students in College and it was hoped by 1962 there would be a total of 400 students, of whom 150 would be men.

The old-style lectures of the '50s (*above*) only had to change style slightly in order to accommodate the men. In other aspects of College life it was more difficult. In the hostels, Betty Murray recalled, the men found community life difficult, with "jazz-fiends" getting out of hand and playing till 2am, ignoring all silence rules. Peace was eventually restored when the men themselves asked for a resident warden and some enforceable rules. This was achieved "*with a bit of stiffening from the work side, as the jazz players were not being satisfactory in the lecture room*"!

Drama was deliberately used in order to integrate the men.

In 1961 *Murder in the Cathedral* (**left**) was staged because it provided men with key roles. It caused some resentment among the women who now had to compete more fiercely for the female roles. But the mixed cast brought a welcome realism to productions and led eventually to a series of excellent Gilbert and Sullivan productions.

On 6th June, 1958, Sir Edward Boyle, Under-secretary for Education, visited College to commemorate the opening of the new student hostels.

Left: **Sir Edward Boyle, Miss Murray and members of the College Council. Bishop Roger Wilson makes his first official appearance, following the death of Bishop George Bell.**

Below left: **Sir Edward Boyle contemplates the mysteries of clay modelling.**

Below: **Inside the new study bedrooms each student has tea-making and washing facilities.**

The new student hostels were completed by September 1957 and provided 56 bed-sits, replacing the old dormitory cubicles, and a warden's flat. Farewell parties were held at the end of the previous summer term in the old dormitories. On the following day the "coffin" wardrobes and iron bedsteads were carried out and the builders started tearing down the old wooden partitions in order to convert the area into teaching units and staff studies.

Sir Edward Boyle's visit was relaxed and informal. He saw all the College and clearly enjoyed himself, with the result that he was able to bend the ear of the Ministry in favour of the College. The Ministry agreed that a major building programme could now go ahead, to provide a new chapel, a dining hall and other important accommodation, with 75% of the cost to be provided by central government.

The need for a larger chapel became apparent in the mid-50s and a proposal for a totally new structure was put forward in 1956-7. A special sub-committee was formed in 1958 to attend to the details. £31,834 was provided by the Ministry of Education. The College governors were very aware that the great expansion of students nationally was a challenge to be met by the Church Colleges. The new chapel was therefore to be prominent and central to the expanding College campus. Working to a tight budget the strikingly-simple design of a square four gabled steel tent was decided upon, typifying the early biblical concept of God's house as a tabernacle.

It was to open on to a central paved and colonnaded court, sharing with it the dining and assembly halls and the students' common room. The Principal, Betty Murray, welcomed the prospect with the following words: *"Sad as I am that we must cease to use the old chapel, I am glad that this enforced move makes it possible to build the new chapel in the very centre of the College where it will stand as a constant reminder that we are a Church foundation with a part to play in the extension of Christ's kingdom"* (Magazine, 1959).

The architect of the new chapel was Peter Shepheard of Bridgwater, Shepheard and Epstein and it was built by Robert Marriott Ltd.

Left and Below: **Aspects of the Dedication Ceremony, 21 March 1962 conducted by Roger Wilson, Bishop of Chichester, in the presence of members of Council, staff, students, representatives of former students, the architects and the builders.**

At 2.15 p.m. the Congregation shall assemble in the Chapel.

At 2.25 p.m. the College Choir shall proceed in procession to its place in the gallery.

The doors of the Chapel shall then be closed.

At 2.30 p.m. the Lord Bishop of Chichester, accompanied by the Archdeacon and attended by his Chaplain, shall be received at the West door of the Chapel by the Principal accompanied by the Dean of Chapel and the College Chaplain.

The Principal shall pray the Bishop to dedicate the Chapel: Reverend Father in God, we pray you to dedicate this Chapel.

To which the Bishop shall reply: I am ready to proceed to the Dedication.

The Bishop shall then knock three times on the closed doors with his Pastoral Staff, and shall say: Open to me the gates of righteousness: that I may go into them, and give thanks unto the Lord. Lift up your heads, O ye gates, and be ye lift up, ye everlasting doors: and the King of Glory shall come in.

Answer shall be made from within by the Congregation: Who is the King of Glory?

The Bishop shall reply: It is the Lord strong and mighty: even the Lord of Hosts, He is the King of Glory.

Left: **The west front of the new chapel showing the abstract aluminium sculpture by Geoffrey Clarke.**

It was intended as a freely expressive piece designed to liberate the viewer's mind within the theme of creation.

Illumination; inspiration; light; kindling of mind and spirit; vision.

These were the words used by the artist himself to describe his feelings about the piece.

Below: **Christmas candle-lit carol service c. 1981. The chaplain Rev. Martin Roberts, with children reading a lesson.**

When the new chapel opened an appeal for £4,000 was already under way. This had paid for enlarging the organ and it was also to pay for a proper altar tapestry. The appeal fund was augmented by concerts held in the new chapel, a custom that continued, once started (See page 114).

The response of the old students to the appeal was, in Betty Murray's words "most generous". Through the appeal, she noted, "those who worshipped in the old chapel are now identified with the new" (Report, 1961-2).

Another link with the old chapel was that the silver cross and candle sticks designed by Gerald Benny and donated to the old chapel by former students in memory of Miss Stella Westaway, vice-principal (1897-1936), were brought into use in the new chapel.

Above Right: **A screen print designed and executed by students Freda Jackson, Maureen Quaintance and Daphne Wright was in place for the dedication ceremony.**

Right: **The new altar tapestry was designed by Jean Lurçat and woven at Aubusson in France.**

He described his work as a great circle with rays issuing from it, like a sun. In it and around it were *all the marvels of creation: water, leaves, rocks, animals, stars. From this creation rises a great flame, going right up to the top of the panel, a flame which has very much appealed to Christians and Theologians… because it conveys very clearly how all created themes are moved to turn towards the sky in worship.*

Above: As well as a second gym and a students' common room, the 1959-61 building programme provided a new **dining hall**. This was most welcome, as previously meals had to be taken in two sittings.

Below: **Bazeley Court.**

The numbers of students continued to rise through the '60s with 471 in 1964 and 609 by 1967. A second building programme provided a music room, a new hall and out-students accommodation. The courtyard in front of the latter was named Bazeley Court, after the former principal. In the few months after it opened it had already served as a venue for an art exhibition, a barbecue, a folk concert and a dance. (Report 1967-8).

Left: **Hockey, 1953.**

Centre left: **Men in residence in New Hall.**

Bottom Left: **Men's cricket, 1970s.**

The transition from an old-fashioned, all-female, to a mixed college was nowhere so marked as on the sports field. After 1957 the hockey pitch had to double as a rugby pitch. The women's cricket team battled on for a while and was, in 1961, still active while a men's team had been formed, played only one match and lost. In 1960 an inter-collegiate netball match resulted in Bishop Otter College and Bognor College trying for first place!

Betty Murray, in reflecting on the problems of the College becoming co-educational found that games had really helped the men "to pull together and feel at home." This, however, caused hard feelings among the women who felt that the men, who were numerically still in the minority, were getting more than their fair share of funds for equipment. All was solved eventually, however, by a compromise whereby the men got an initial grant to help launch their clubs, with the continuing expenses to be financed out of union funds.

By 1970 Betty Murray was about to leave the College she had helped to transform. Her achievement was that the College had kept pace in two decades of rapid social change.

The students' social life was now centred on union activities and the old College clubs and societies had been officially disbanded. Politics and current affairs, including the cry for nuclear disarmament, had a high profile among student activities, and obtained a platform in the new pacey magazine entitled *Otters' Utter* (later simply *Otter*) which started publication in 1958. The old-fashioned annual magazine died a few years later, though much of its interesting and thoughtful style of content has continued to this day in *The Guild Chronicle* which started in 1951.

Though the architectural styles of the new College buildings were "sixties", the architectural ideals were timeless. The new complex promoted the following praise from architectural historians.

… the sensitivity of the roof lines and enclosure of space is outstanding..
(I. Nairn and N. Pevsner, The Buildings of England, Sussex, p 173).

The courtyard complexes provided space, yet intimacy, for formal and informal gatherings and, through a series of walkways, were linked to the old College of which they were now an integral part.

Left: **Chapel courtyard looking back to the Edwardian wings of the College, 1970s.**

Chapter 10.
THE '70s AND '80`s

In 1973, in response to a government "White Paper" - **Education, a framework for Expansion**, (December 1972) the possibility of providing a campus for 1200 students was discussed. Talks were tentatively initiated by the academic board with Bognor College on the future of higher education in West Sussex.

In reality it was not expansion but contraction that dictated the College's immediate future. There was a falling birth-rate and the government was unwilling to invest in smaller class sizes. By 1975 this had caused the Council of Church Training Colleges to present a plan for cutting the number of their colleges from 27 to 18. Bishop Otter College was not among the 18 to be saved.

In July 1975 West Sussex County Council approved the idea of an Institute of Higher Education based on Bognor College, with links to Bishop Otter and Chichester College of Further Education. The scheme was rejected by the D.E.S.

Pressing on in what was, by then, a very serious situation for Bishop Otter College, a Board of Education Working Party acknowledged that the College was the most popular of the Church colleges and therefore merited a reprieve. It decided that a new scheme for merger with the Local Education Authority College, Bognor College, seemed to offer possibilities and, though not ideal, was workable. In October 1975 the Board of Education, and in November 1975, the Church Synod, accepted the proposal. The merger took place in 1976. Bishop Otter College and Bognor Regis College, while maintaining their two separate campuses, became one body, the West Sussex Institute of Higher Education. John Wyatt, Principal of Cullam College, which did not escape closure, became the Director of the new Institute.

Reflecting on the event the following year, Gordon McGregor shared with former students his hopes for the future of the College.

The College has survived many crises in the past and my research on its history convinces me that our present problems and anxieties, though not trivial, are not to be compared with for example the years of survival through two world wars and the actual closure of the College in 1867. We have much to be grateful for, not least the support and encouragement of so many former students who want to see the best that they know at Bishop Otter preserved. We shall do all in our power to see that it is.

(Guild Newsletter, May 1977)

Dr. Gordon McGregor was Principal from 1970 -1977 and Head of College until 1981. He thus presided over the College's final years of autonomy, steering it, with care, into the new W.S.I.H.E.. He has bequeathed a generous memorial to the College and its history in his research study published as *Bishop Otter College and Policy for Teacher Education, 1839 - 1980.*

An audio-visual department was established in College in the late '60s. In the '70s this was developed as an important part of the educational programme to support the work of the education department. It gradually built up a wide range of photographic, reprographic and audio-visual equipment which were freely available for use by persons in the college.

Right and centre: **Rugby football received a fillip in the '70s by virtue of the fact that the Principal himself was a player; but the 80 year old tradition of hockey was still alive and well.**

Below: **Sporting activities had diversified to include mountaineering (in Snowdonia 1978), and athletics.**

Above: **The new art and craft wing was complete by Spring 1971, with the music block (detached octagon) a few years its senior.**

True to a long-standing College tradition it offered experience in ceramics and sculpture, weaving, fabric printing and print-making as well as fine art. Today the Related Arts degree offers an imaginative mix of the different artistic disciplines of music, art, dance and english.

Below: **Weaving in the new art and craft wing, 1970s.**

Above: **Out-students' building, early '70s. This is now the Dance Studio and the Students' Union offices and bar.**

Below: Students relaxing in the **late '70s and the '80s.**

The conflict between students' personal freedom and community life was energetically addressed in the early '70s by a new Community Affairs Council. Composed of staff and students, it aimed to be less exclusive than the Joint Representative Council it replaced. A poll taken in 1973 found that the overwhelming opinion was in favour of campus residence, despite its shortcomings.

Above: **Street play at Chichester Cross, as part of the Foundation Course, December 1977.**

True to tradition, the College continued to make its contribution to the wider community during the '70s. In 1978 and 1979 Rag week, though silly, outrageous and extreme, scaled the heights in fund raising under Rag Chairman, Richard Geffen. Donations were made to numerous local causes including the R.N.I.B., Research into Spina Bifida and Cystic Fibrosis, and to the Aldingbourne Horticultural Trust for the mentally handicapped.

Centre: **Tarts competition, 1978.**

Left: **Chairman Richard Geffen with Drag Queen and Tarts Queen Pete Bell and Lou Parr at the cheques presentation ceremony, 1979.**

Below: **Rag week, 1980. The Chairman this year was Duncan Hamer.**

Above: **Michael Waite, head of music, conducting the Institute's choir and a chamber orchestra in the Chapel.**

During the '80s the Chapel (*above left*) continued its central role in College life and provided a stage for drama, debate, orchestral and choral events, as well as the divine service, with the students taking an active part in running the chapel and its services under the guidance of 3 successive chaplains - John Young, Martin Roberts and Ken Woolhouse.

Below: **The opening of the Murray Hall: 3 July 1982. (Dr. Murray with flowers). Peter Toyne (Head of College) standing with his wife Angela. Seated in front, Miss Howell, former member of staff. The gathering includes 11 members of the 1932 year group.**

Dr. McGregor left Bishop Otter College in July 1980 in order to take up a post as Principal of Ripon and York St. John's College.

He was succeeded as Head of College by Peter Toyne (see below opposite page). In 1983 he left to become Deputy Director of N. E. London Polytechnic and is now Principal of Liverpool Polytechnic.

Each of the 2 campuses of the new Institute of Higher Education specialised in certain subjects. On the Bishop Otter campus Sports Studies and Science Studies were able to take advantage of good facilities built up over previous years.

The Murray Hall (*left*) was built as an assembly hall. It was provided with a stage and dressing rooms which allowed it to be used for plays and performances by Opera '70 under the direction of Michael Waite.

Top Right. Sports Studies students use scientific methods to test physical endurance.

Bottom Right: Teaching practise in schools was aided by mobile audio-visual units that the students took with them; this helped teachers and children alike to develop new learning methods.

In the late '60s and early '70s the challenge for the library was to meet the needs of an expanded campus: and in the '80s to keep abreast of technological change.

A Library and Resources Committee was added to the Academic Board in 1971 and temporary relief for cramped accommodation was found by overflowing into the out-students' block.

Pressure was somewhat eased after 1977 when the BOC campus of the Institute concentrated only on the subjects taught there and the library followed suit. During the '80s the library was constantly modernised and updated in its service, providing slides, video-cassettes, audio-cassettes, computer software and compact discs, while search and retrieval was simplified by computerisation.

The Chichester and Graylingwell School of Nursing was based at Bishop Otter College in 1985, bringing its own stock of books to be added to the library along with specialist library staff. In 1989 the School of Nursing was merged with the Worthing School of Nursing and renamed the West Sussex College of Nursing and Midwifery.

In 1988 the library combined with the Media Resources Department and the Information Technology development to form a new Learning Resources Unit.

In 1987 'Jock' Johnston, Principal Librarian since 1972, retired and was replaced by Scott Robertson as Learning Resources Co-ordinator. The library now has upward of 90,000 books.

Right: **Preparing for the new Senior Common Room 1981. Gerry Abery, the College Estates Manager, measures for the new bay window.**

Below: The opening of the new SCR by John Wyatt (standing to the right of the central trio) in 1983. To the left stand Martin Roberts (chaplain) and John Rankin (head of religious studies and later mayor of Chichester). Behind John Wyatt is Philip Morris (geography and later human movement studies). In the new bay window, holding a handbag, is 'Jock' Johnson the librarian.

The College students in July 1989, 150 years after the death of the founder.

Chapter 11.

THE 150th CELEBRATIONS
OCTOBER 1989 - OCTOBER 1990

In the Presence of H.R.H. the Princess Royal
The Chairman and Council of the Church College Principals
request the pleasure of the company of

.... Dr. J.T. Brighton ....

at a Luncheon to commemorate 150 years of Church of England
Colleges, at Church House, on Thursday, 7th December 1989,
from 12.00 to 2.30 pm.

12.00 pm for 12.30 pm
Sherry and Welcome:
Bishop Partridge Hall
No Admittance after 12.30 pm
1.00 pm *Buffet Luncheon:*
Hoare Memorial Hall

Lounge Suits

RSVP *Mr. Michael Chater*
Colleges' Officer
Board of Education
Church House
Great Smith Street
London SW1P 3NZ

by 28th November 1989

Please bring this card with you

THE SESQUICENTENNIAL CELEBRATIONS

As early as 1986 it was decided to celebrate the College's 150th anniversary with a year of celebrations starting at the beginning of October 1989 and ending in the following October 1990. This would enable the decision to establish a college in December 1839 and its actual opening in April 1840 to be commemorated. Furthermore, there would be ample time for all the academic sections to arrange open days, exhibitions and a variety of cultural events.

The year opened with the arrival of the sculptor in residence, John Skelton, closely followed by two huge blocks of stone which he and his apprentice, Giles Wright, were to fashion into 'Axis Mundi'. Lectures and concerts followed and new compositions were performed. Works of art were commissioned and purchased for the College collection.

Services were held in the College chapel, Chichester Cathedral and Westminster Abbey. The last occasion was one of celebration by all the Church Colleges when the Archbishop of Canterbury preached on their contributions to education. At a subsequent reception in Church House, Trevor Brighton presented Princess Anne with the commemorative book he had edited, **'150 Years: the Church Colleges in Higher Education'. (Above right).**

The College Art collection and the Mitre Gallery

The College was expanding and changing rapidly as it entered the West Sussex Institute of Higher Education in 1977. More of the public came into the College and security for the Art Collection increasingly became a problem. As early as 1959 the collection's small seated figure in bronze by Henry Moore was stolen. This was replaced by his *Seated Figure on Square Steps*. Then in July 1983 seven pictures were stolen from the walls of the College and taken to California for sale. In the following September, Dr. Trevor Brighton arrived as Head of College to find the collection and its curatorial committee in total disarray. The police gave strong advice against the old method of displaying the collection and the College's insurance company threatened prohibitive premiums.

Fortunately, the FBI found the stolen pictures and returned them, but the valuable items of the collection remained locked away. Trevor Brighton, who had curatorial responsibility, had to take pictures from their racks, one at a time, to see them. He had been Dean of the Faculty of Art and Design at Sheffield City Polytechnic where he had the care of a fine gallery for the exhibition of the Faculty's standing collection, students' work and that of contemporary artists. A gallery could be the solution to the College's problems and would certainly satisfy the insurers.

In 1987 he began to press the Institute Governors and the College Trustees to provide a gallery and to allow purchase for the collection once more by giving an increased annual allowance. In 1988 Alice Kettle's hanging **Harlequin Madonna** was purchased and then in 1990, to celebrate the College's 150th anniversary, the new Mitre Gallery was opened by Richard Luce MP, Minister for the Arts. The occasion was graced by much of the College's collection being on exhibition together with a new acquisition **Wagner** by David Hockney.

A second, smaller space, known as the Cloister Gallery, was also opened to exhibit student work throughout the year and an annual prize was awarded for outstanding work by a student in College. The prize-winning work each year is now added to the collection.

In 1990 also, two other notable additions were made. Trevor Brighton, on behalf of the Governors, appointed John Skelton, OBE, sculptor in residence. His **Axis Mundi**, sculpted in stone outdoors, was dedicated by Archdeacon Filby following Graduation Day in Chichester Festival Theatre.

The second addition was the bequest of the Archdeacon of Chichester, Lancelot Mason. This consisted of a collection of ceramics, including figurines by Audrey Blackman, and a gift of £500. The money was used to purchase a display case for the collection.

Left: The new Mitre Gallery is opened by the Rt Hon. Richard Luce MP, Minister for the Arts, 18 January 1990. Left to right: Richard Luce, Chairman of Governors, Mrs Margaret Johnson, Head of College Dr. Trevor Brighton and Governor Mr Stanley Elliot. (Photograph by courstesy of the Chichester Observer)

The year of celebrations reached a crescendo at the weekend of 15th to 17th July 1990. This amazingly successful occasion was superbly organised by Dr. Graham Stodd, a tutor in the College for 25 years assisted by his wife Angela, an old student (née Anson).

All the rooms in College were booked; caravans arrived on the south field and tents were pitched on the north. Local hotel accommodation was taken as "Old Otters" returned to their holt. Some had not trodden the College cloisters since their farewell, in some cases in the 1930s. "Old contemptibles" and young graduates, many with their husbands and wives and some with their children, mingled and reminisced.

Welcomes extended throughout Friday afternoon. Dinner was served in the refectory and afterwards came a lecture! No one took notes and there was much laughter as Dr. John Fines, head of history, reflected lightheartedly on a century and a half of teacher training in Church Colleges.

College bars opened and a thousand individual histories - biographies and autobiographies – were recited into the early hours.

On Saturday morning the whole College was open to the visitors and demonstrations and exhibitions occupied classrooms and corridors. Most popular was the display of manuscripts, prints, photographs, paintings and artifacts mounted by Heather Warne, the College archivist, in the Mitre Gallery. The College is, indeed, well endowed in its excellent collections. Mugshots of old worthies, clergy, ministers of state and royalty mingled with those of students over the years – all watched over by the kindly William Otter whose bust welcomed all as they entered.

The weather for the reunion was idyllic throughout the weekend. Before lunch on that glorious Saturday hordes of visitors in shirt sleeves and floral frocks trooped to six different venues to drink a toast to *Alma Mater* and to wish her well in the years ahead. Then staff old and new, with their principal guest, Dr. Betty Murray, dined in the refectory and the alumni took to the lawns, marquees and arbours and picnicked to the popping of corks and the clicking of cameras.

The evening bought revelries under the stars as music reverberated through cloister and garden. The dance band of the Royal Artillery produced a "big-band" sound in the Murray Hall and a jazz band entertained the youngest and most lively in Bazeley Court. For the more sedate the restrained tones of a trio accompanied cocktails, coffee and gentle conversation in the Senior Common Room. Dinner was taken in shifts in the refectory and the marquee in the Chapel courtyard.

Above: **Student helpers at the l50th revelries.**

Below: **1) Dancing in the Murray Hall to the Royal Artillery "Big Band".**
2) Relaxing in the Senior Common Room to gentle music.
(Most of the photographs of the Reunion were taken by Dr. Tony Barnes)

Above and Below: **Jazzing it in Bazeley Court.**

Above: **Refreshments.**

Right: **A well earned rest for the two master-minds of the 150th, Dr. Trevor Brighton (left), and Dr. Graham Stodd (right).**

Below: Several group photos of former students were taken during the weekend of which there is regrettably, only space here for one. These are the " 1942 and earlier" students.

Despite the late retirement to bed of many on Saturday night, the College Chapel was packed on Sunday morning for the celebration of communion by Dr. Eric Kemp, Bishop of Chichester. The central place of the Church and worship in William Otter's foundation had not been forgotten.

And so to farewells. Some stayed to a valedictory barbecue in the grounds. Others, nostalgic to the last, threw off their years and joined a crowd who walked to the top of the Trundle, as they had - and all new students still do - on their first coming to Bishop Otter College. Among them, and epitomising much of the spirit of the old students, was the redoubtable Betty Murray.

The finale of the year's festivities took place on Graduation Day, Saturday 6 October 1990. John Skelton, OBE, sculptor in residence at the College for the past year, joined it in a double celebration. First, his daughter Rebecca had graduated that day and afterwards his **Axis Mundi**, sculpted outdoors in French limestone, was dedicated by Archdeacon William Filby.

The mind flashed back to the beginning of this *annus mirabilis* and John Skelton's opening lecture about his proposed sculpture. His drawings of a tau-cross form, symbolising the history, spirit and faith of the College community over a century and a half, had now become a reality - aligned, on its mound, with the axis of the Chapel. The mind now flashes forward in time and sees the **Axis Mundi** as a symbol of William Otter's vision of the future.

Chapter 12.
EPILOGUE

ON LEAVING COLLEGE

Wistaria now is dream-decked with fair bloom,
A dim rich glory on the old grey stone;
In proudest splendour stands the Turkey Oak,
The Deodar towers lofty and alone.
It seems that Beauty comes to meet us here,
Beauty in songs of birds, in flowers and trees,
Beauty that while we live must haunt us still,
Haunt, as the murmur of far distant seas.
Beauty in books, in friends, in youth, in life.
And, as we journey through the changeful years,
Sweet Downland memories bring peace from far,
The hush of Nature's peace which nought can mar.

L.E. COE.

College Magazine, June 1925

The timeless charm of the lawn.

Above: Prize-giving on Sports Day, 1918.

Below: "Valediction", 1970s.

The Cloisters

Left: The cloisters in 1923 (from **Elaine Brogatski's archive**).

Right: The cloisters in 1979 before the creation of the Senior Common Room and insertion of glass in door and windows in 1984.

The Turkey Oak

Above: Open Day 1932. Country dancing round the Turkey oak.

Right: Country dancing in the 1980s round the Turkey oak.

Dance, dance, wherever you may be.......

Above: **Movement and expression, 1940.**

Below: **Minerva Madness, 1989. Photograph kindly lent by Chris Butler,
senior lecturer in dance.**

"I have been young, and now am old; yet have I not seen the righteous forsaken"
Ps 37 V. 25.

I have been young, and now am old. I suppose that any reunion makes us feel that way. What should be said about it? Well, I was wandering round the grounds of Bishop Otter College the other day, with my dog, reflecting on what I might say to you today, when my theme suddenly came into my vision. For some time the marble bust of Bishop Otter had been separated from its pedestal in the garden. I saw that it had been replaced, and in going to look at it I noticed for the first time the words written on the pedestal, "Time goes, Friendship stays." Here, I saw, was the theme for a sermon at a College reunion. "Time goes". Of that inescapable truth the College buildings themselves give us a vivid reminder. Anyone walking round can see at a glance the passage of time as marked by the successive stages from the old stone cloister to the new aluminium spire of the Chapel. There are people here who can remember, as I do, the opening of New Hall, but today New Hall seems almost as oddly named as the New Forest, since there are now so many newer buildings. Time and change have certainly left their mark upon the outward aspect of the College, but it is the same College.

'I have been young, and now am old ', but it is still me.

From the address by Lancelot Mason, Archdeacon of Chichester at the Summer Reunion, 1965.

The 150 years since the death of William Otter, Bishop of Chichester, have seen an untiring stream of energy and enthusiasm for carrying his dream into a reality. The Bishop was a visionary, ahead of his time. His desire for "education for all" could not be fulfilled overnight: but his College has played its part towards achieving that end. It stands, and will stand in the future, as a monument to his name.